AF604630

Anxiety-Free Journal

Breathe

90 DAYS
TO SUCCESS

Introduction

NOTE TO THE READER:

The types of stress and anxiety discussed in this journal are not prolonged or survival-related but the ubiquitous kind that pervade our everyday lives. If you're having trouble with extreme stress and anxiety, please take care of yourself and seek professional support.

It's hard not to feel anxious these days. Life is fast, with more and more inputs seemingly demanding attention (ding, ding, ding, go the notifications on our phones). The constant comparison to others on social media means that there is never a lack of things we're told we need to do, be or have.

If you've picked up this journal, it's likely you find yourself struggling to some degree with the pressures of daily life. You are not alone. Stress is something most of us try our best to manage day-by-day.

The good news is that although we can't always control the external stressors in life, we can balance their effects on our physical body, reflect on their causes and learn ways to prime ourselves to roll with these challenging periods. In short, we can learn tools to combat anxiety.

Most of all, we can pause and breathe: that is, stop what we are thinking or doing, and take a moment to reset. When we pause, we make a conscious choice to look after ourselves and acknowledge that we have the power to adjust the outcome in any given moment. The pause is an invitation to let go of the chattering of the monkey mind, be still, be present and be real. The breath is the body's gift to help us manage that process physiologically – it is calming and restorative, and slows us down.

If your mind is overflowing with what to do next and you feel you don't know how to support yourself properly, the daily reflection prompts in this meditation journal will guide you to create simple habits that bring comfort and clarity of mind.

How This Journal Works

Knowledge is power. Getting a detailed picture of what your life looks like for 90 days will help you to forge a clear path towards a renewed, more relaxed way of being.

Fill in one journal spread a day for 90 days, following the carefully designed prompts that help you notice where stress occurs in your life and find opportunities to pause. In doing so, you'll learn how to lessen the impacts of stress both in the moment and in the future.

Ninety days is the perfect amount of time: not so long that it's daunting, but long enough for you to instil positive habits and create lasting change. And the reward at the end is worth the effort: a greater understanding of how stress feels in your body and mind, and a range of positive tools to help balance its effects.

Filling It In

Put your reflections into context by noting the date and day of the week (Mondays can be hard for some of us!), plus a simple 'word of the day' that captures how you feel.

Each fill-in journal spread is divided into four columns: Check In, Reflect, Pause and Connect. You can learn more about how to fill in these columns on pages 6-21.

Ideally, you should complete your journal in the evening before bed, to reflect on your day.

When you have finished your entry for the day, take a moment to write down something that you're grateful for. Even if your day has been a challenging one, there is likely some small moment that you can give thanks for.

Engaging and reflecting upon your day-to-day life with honesty and respect for your own limits and challenges will help you to identify how you can truly flourish.

Refer to the sample journal entry on pages 22–23 for ideas and inspiration.

Check In

Anxiety can seek to consume our bodies as it does our minds, and ultimately, our days. In the spin of things we forget: it is *your* body and *your* mind, and *you* are in control. Fill in the daily journal prompts to check in with yourself.

To begin, pause and connect with your body. Take a deep breath, closing your eyes if possible – and mentally scan from head to toe.

Are you feeling tired or slow, energised or strong? Are there any niggles or pain that you didn't notice in the rush of the day?

How does this compare to yesterday – do you feel better or worse? Take your time, and then circle or write down the body-feeling that aligns for you. (Or use the space provided to write your own.)

A body scan is an excellent way to take a mindful moment at the end of your day – especially if it was a stressful one. Why not try combining it with a short meditation or a gentle stretch?

Next, reflect on your feelings throughout the day. What was your dominant emotion? Consider this and then circle your mood from the list or write in your own.

As the days go by, you can begin to use this 'data' that you are collecting about yourself. Comb back through each entry after 10, 20 and 30 days, and see if you can spot trends and patterns over the course of the 90-day journey.

Is your anxiety influenced by external factors? Is it dependant on the day of the week, the people you interact with, the weather or the pace of your schedule? Does it dip mid-week and pick up towards the weekend? Are your weekends too quiet or weekdays too loud? Examine these patterns with compassion and interest (and without judgement), and let your observations empower you to make positive changes for the future.

Review your stress signals during the day, and give yourself a rating. The stress signals you will rank in this journal are quality of the breath (slow and smooth or fast and jagged), state of mind (calm or busy), focus (easy or hard to concentrate) and ability to switch off (easy or challenging).

Consider how your answers to these questions relate to the other information you've recorded in this column. If you're feeling peaceful, it's likely your breathing will be slow. If you're feeling frustrated or sad, you might be finding it hard to concentrate. Circle the level that applies or tick a box in the middle if you're feeling somewhere in between.

Finally, shade in your 'score' on the stress danger rating. Was today a 'keeping it cool' day, a 'red hot rage' day or something in the middle?

Remember not to assign blame, shame or judgement – your job is simply to observe.

Use this page to reflect on how your body reacts to stress.

How do you know when you're stressed?
What behaviours do you tend to default to?

Reflect

In this section, you'll review an anxiety-provoking situation that occurred during your day and reflect on it, employing some anxiety-busting techniques to help you. (If nothing comes to mind on a given day, that's amazing. Hold onto those good days like armour, buffering your resilience for the inevitable ups and downs to come. Acknowledge your sweet day and send out a high five to the universe.)

But maybe your day 'had its moments'. That's ok. They often do.

First, briefly recount the stressful moment. Where and when did it happen? Who was involved? Then, reflect on why it challenged you. Did the way you were feeling at the time make a difference – perhaps you were rushing, tired or distracted? Had something happened earlier in the day that impacted your mood? Use the space in your daily journal to record this situation and your reflections.

An important technique you can use to reflect on a stressful moment is something called 'Turn the story around'. It's just a story, after all. The stories we tell ourselves about people or situations play a big role in how we feel about them and even in the outcomes – and you can absolutely influence this.

Here's a simple example. You've had a piece of chocolate and now you want another piece, and you can't relax until you have one. Your mind is jibbering at you about wanting more. Turn the story around. Instead of denying yourself, reward yourself for your choice. You could change the mental story to: 'I have the chance to enjoy a piece of chocolate *and* feel good about honouring my body and treating it with respect'. Plus, you get the added bonus of the mental strength that comes with knowing temptation can be resisted – on your terms. Experiment with this technique and experience the power of turning the story around.

Next imagine your yourself viewing the situation from a different perspective. You could think of yourself as being physically above it, looking down on the scene. What can you see? Or you could imagine what your best mate might say. Record this 'bird's-eye view' of the situation and see if it offers you any insights or comfort.

Two other important tools that you can use to help manage anxiety in the moment are breathing and leaving. In this section, you can reflect on which of those tools you used or note another tool that works for you.

Breathing is magic when it comes to stress management. It works by slowing your heart rate and stimulating the vagus nerve, part of the parasympathetic nervous system. Triggering this system helps you calm down, feel better and think more clearly.

Try changing the ratio of your inhale to exhale. This breathwork approach is commonly used to reduce stress. When you inhale, your heart rate speeds up. When you exhale, it slows down.

Another important tool in managing a situation that makes you anxious is to leave and do something else instead (if you can). Don't sit with your fear like a deer in headlights. Go for a walk. Make a cup of tea. Drink a hydrating glass of water. Stand on one leg for 30 seconds. You are back in control.

When anxiety strikes, if you can find a way to integrate a moment of reflection and use some of these tools for self-control, you will have built a powerful and empowering new habit.

Before you get started, complete the questions on the following pages, which will help you explore your current reactions when anxiety strikes.

What are your stress triggers? Can you identify particular people or events that provoke anxiety in you? Why is that?

Which of the stress tools mentioned in the previous pages (turn the story around, birds eye view, breathing and leaving) resonate most with you and why?

Pause

Some things help us cope with anxiety, while others intensify it. That's a simple fact. Here you'll explore how to use the power of pausing and breathing to decrease the negative impacts of stress in your life in certain areas.

Whenever something stressful happens around us or to us, there's a moment where we can pause and choose before we respond.

Let's take social media – it's a biggie for most of us. 'I feel so great after 30 minutes engaging with social media', said no-one ever! Most of us come away feeling anxious that we aren't doing, having or being enough. Gah. Why do we do it to ourselves? Consider how pausing and breathing can provide you with the opportunity to make a different decision for yourself.

Try this instead: when you reach for your phone or tablet, instead of clicking on your socials, go to your notes app and write down three things you are grateful for. Now put down your device and walk away. Do something else.

Take a moment to record your experiences in the journal prompts and enjoy the feel-good satisfaction that comes from making a positive choice and expressing gratitude – a double whammy. You feel better, right?

Anxiety lives in the future – it's worry about what's to come. It can feel like a constant mental rollercoaster that won't stop. But you can change that. Pausing and breathing is stopping. It's heading off that thought at the pass, and redirecting it somewhere that's better for you. This is a skill that you can learn with the help of the prompts in this section of the journal. Let's call this your 'mindfulness pause'.

Central to the mindfulness pause is the notion of bringing yourself back to the here and now, the present moment. In the present moment, we can experience our lives, rather than constantly preparing for what's next. Keep in your heart the words of Zen Master Thich Nhat Hanh: "Breathing in, I calm my body. Breathing out, I smile. Dwelling in the present moment, I know this is a wonderful moment."

You can use your mindfulness pause whenever you want – set a timer to do it hourly or reserve it for stressful moments. The choice is yours, but when completing this journal aim for at least one mindfulness pause each day. Work out what is achievable for you. If it's a minute sitting and focusing on your breathing – that's wonderful. If it's 15 minutes of meditation, that's great too. Write down how you feel before and after that moment of calm.

Record any shift in your anxiety levels that you noticed after taking a pause by giving yourself a score out of 10 before and after you employed this technique.

Moving and stretching your body helps diffuse the stress response, bringing you out of your head and into the present moment. It also creates motivation and energy. When stress and anxiety creep in, you have the power to get up and go out. Go for a big walk, do a down dog or dance around the kitchen for five minutes. This tells your body that it is safe, away from the 'stressor' and helps it relax. Track what movement worked for you, and aim to do it more often.

To set yourself up for success in this section of the journal, use the following spread to reflect on your understanding of 'pausing and breathing' and how this can be applied to help you better manage your anxiety.

Reflect on a situation where taking a pause could have been useful or when you may have taken a pause unknowingly. How did it affect the situation? (take those learnings with you over the next 90 days.)

What strategies do you use to get back to the present moment?

Connect

Connection with others is important for a healthy, anxiety-free life. Strong relationships not only help us to maintain a positive mindset, warding off anxiety and depression, but they also support our physical body and immune system. In this section, you'll take a little time each day to journal about positive moments of connection.

Connections with others don't always have to be two-way (such as deep and meaningful conversations with a partner or loved one) – acts of service and caring for someone else have also been shown to reduce the impacts of stress.

There's also a lot to be said for the small, quiet connections that happen in the 'in-between' moments: a friendly greeting to a stranger on the train or a brief chat about the weather with a neighbour. In fact, connection doesn't even have to be with another human – connecting with mother nature or furry friends counts, too.

In the first journal prompt, you will list three moments of connection that you experienced during the day.

Write down your moments and take time to reflect on each one. What were you doing before the moment? How did it feel when you connected? How did you feel immediately after? Were you able to carry that connected feeling with you for the rest of the day or was it easily overshadowed by another stressor? Taking time to first identify and then record these moments of connection will help you notice them in the future, and keep them front of mind.

Tiny, beautiful moments of connection happen more often than we think. They're a kind of self-fulfilling prophecy: the more we acknowledge them, the more moments there will be.

Gratitude helps train our minds to make a habit of finding the silver lining in the gloomiest of days. Take a moment to note a relationship that you're grateful for and why. It can be somebody close to you, the local barista, a distant acquaintance or even somebody you haven't met in real life. If you want a real challenge, try to avoid doubling up on the same person over the course of the 90 days. This will encourage you to expand your awareness of all the different relationships around you.

Sharing your gratitude for the people in your life helps reinforce your connectedness. Saying 'thank you' is free and it makes everybody feel better. If you are not in the habit of using the word liberally, now's your chance to correct that. In the last prompt of this section, take a minute to consider when you said thank you today. Who was it to? How and why did you say it? How did you feel after this acknowledgement?

Before you start your 90-day journey completing this journal, take a moment to answer the questions on the following pages.

Are you happy with the quantity and quality of your close relationships? Are there any gaps in your network that are bothering you? What could you do about that?

Use this space to reflect on your approach to gratitude. (Does it come naturally? Is it intentional? How does it make you feel?)

Word of the day

Growing

DAY M (T) W T F S S

DATE 27 / 11 / 2023

Check-in

Today's body feels

- ENERGETIC
- STRONG
- ACHY
- CAPABLE
- (TIRED) — circled
- SLOW

Today's dominant vibe

- CALM
- OPTIMISTIC
- OKAY
- SAD
- NERVOUS
- SATISFIED
- ANGRY
- (YEAH-NAH) — circled

Today's stress signals

Breathing

SLOW ○ ✓ ○ FAST

Mind

CALM ○ ✓ ○ RACING

Concentration

FOCUSED ○ ✓ ○ DISTRACTED

Switching off

SIMPLE ○ ○ ✓ CHALLENGING

Today's stress danger rating

COOL ← → HOT

Reflect

Stressful moment

Realising I was unprepared for the EOD meeting

Did I 'turn the story around'? How?

This is the first time this has happened - it's OK

Bird's-eye view

Having been here 3 years, 1 hour isn't a big deal

Tools I used

- [x] BREATHE
- [ ] LEAVE
- [ ] MOVE
- [x] OTHER did some tapping

Today, I am feeling good about ...

My ability to catch the story before it spun me out

Pause

Did I do my gratitude notes?

☑ YES ◯ NO

Feeling before

Meh

Feeling after

Lucky

Did I take a mindfulness pause?

☑ YES ◯ NO

Feeling before

Swirly and panicky

Feeling after

More capable

Pausing improved my stress

FROM 5/10 TO 8/10

Connect

3 moments of connection

1. Stories with Frankie at the dinner table
2. Calling Mum on my drive to work
3. A nice 20-minute walk with the dog after work

Person I'm grateful for (and why)

Myself - for committing to this journalling practice

Today's thank you moment

To Tom for looking after the kids so I could go for a solo walk

90 Days

Starts Now

Word of the day

DAY M T W T F S S

DATE / /

Check-in

Today's body feels

- ENERGETIC
- STRONG
- ACHY
- CAPABLE
- TIRED
- SLOW
-

Today's dominant vibe

- CALM
- OPTIMISTIC
- OKAY
- SAD
- NERVOUS
- SATISFIED
- ANGRY
- YEAH-NAH
-

Today's stress signals

Breathing

SLOW ○ ○ ○ FAST

Mind

CALM ○ ○ ○ RACING

Concentration

FOCUSED ○ ○ ○ DISTRACTED

Switching off

SIMPLE ○ ○ ○ CHALLENGING

Today's stress danger rating

COOL ← → HOT

Reflect

Stressful moment

Did I 'turn the story around'? How?

Bird's-eye view

Tools I used

- ☐ BREATHE
- ☐ LEAVE
- ☐ MOVE
- ☐ OTHER

Today, I am feeling good about ...

Pause

Did I do my gratitude notes?

◯ YES ◯ NO

Feeling before

Feeling after

Did I take a mindfulness pause?

◯ YES ◯ NO

Feeling before

Feeling after

Pausing improved my stress

FROM /10

TO /10

Connect

3 moments of connection

1.

2.

3.

Person I'm grateful for (and why)

Today's thank you moment

Word of the day

DAY M T W T F S S

DATE / /

Check-in

Today's body feels

- ENERGETIC
- STRONG
- ACHY
- CAPABLE
- TIRED
- SLOW
-

Today's dominant vibe

- CALM
- OPTIMISTIC
- OKAY
- SAD
- NERVOUS
- SATISFIED
- ANGRY
- YEAH-NAH
-

Today's stress signals

Breathing

SLOW ○ ○ ○ FAST

Mind

CALM ○ ○ ○ RACING

Concentration

FOCUSED ○ ○ ○ DISTRACTED

Switching off

SIMPLE ○ ○ ○ CHALLENGING

Today's stress danger rating

COOL ← → HOT

Reflect

Stressful moment

Did I 'turn the story around'? How?

Bird's-eye view

Tools I used

- ☐ BREATHE
- ☐ LEAVE
- ☐ MOVE
- ☐ OTHER

Today, I am feeling good about ...

Pause

Did I do my gratitude notes?

YES NO

Feeling before

Feeling after

Did I take a mindfulness pause?

YES NO

Feeling before

Feeling after

Pausing improved my stress

FROM /10 TO /10

Connect

3 moments of connection

1.

2.

3.

Person I'm grateful for (and why)

Today's thank you moment

Word of the day

DAY M T W T F S S

DATE / /

Check-in

Today's body feels

Today's dominant vibe

- CALM
- OPTIMISTIC
- OKAY
- SAD
- NERVOUS
- SATISFIED
- ANGRY
- YEAH-NAH

Today's stress signals

Breathing

SLOW ○ ○ ○ FAST

Mind

CALM ○ ○ ○ RACING

Concentration

FOCUSED ○ ○ ○ DISTRACTED

Switching off

SIMPLE ○ ○ ○ CHALLENGING

Today's stress danger rating

COOL ← → HOT

Reflect

Stressful moment

Did I 'turn the story around'? How?

Bird's-eye view

Tools I used

- ☐ BREATHE
- ☐ LEAVE
- ☐ MOVE
- ☐ OTHER

Today, I am feeling good about ...

Pause

Did I do my gratitude notes?

YES NO

Feeling before

Feeling after

Did I take a mindfulness pause?

YES NO

Feeling before

Feeling after

Pausing improved my stress

FROM /10

TO /10

Connect

3 moments of connection

1.

2.

3.

Person I'm grateful for (and why)

Today's thank you moment

Word of the day

DAY M T W T F S S

DATE / /

Check-in

Today's body feels

- ENERGETIC
- STRONG
- ACHY
- CAPABLE
- TIRED
- SLOW
-

Today's dominant vibe

- CALM
- OPTIMISTIC
- OKAY
- SAD
- NERVOUS
- SATISFIED
- ANGRY
- YEAH-NAH
-

Today's stress signals

Breathing

SLOW ○ ○ ○ FAST

Mind

CALM ○ ○ ○ RACING

Concentration

FOCUSED ○ ○ ○ DISTRACTED

Switching off

SIMPLE ○ ○ ○ CHALLENGING

Today's stress danger rating

COOL ← → HOT

Reflect

Stressful moment

Did I 'turn the story around'? How?

Bird's-eye view

Tools I used

- [ ] BREATHE
- [ ] LEAVE
- [ ] MOVE
- [ ] OTHER

Today, I am feeling good about ...

Pause

Did I do my gratitude notes?

YES NO

Feeling before

Feeling after

Did I take a mindfulness pause?

YES NO

Feeling before

Feeling after

Pausing improved my stress

FROM /10

TO /10

Connect

3 moments of connection

1.

2.

3.

Person I'm grateful for (and why)

Today's thank you moment

Word of the day

DAY M T W T F S S

DATE / /

Check-in

Today's body feels

- ENERGETIC
- STRONG
- ACHY
- CAPABLE
- TIRED
- SLOW
-

Today's dominant vibe

- CALM
- OPTIMISTIC
- OKAY
- SAD
- NERVOUS
- SATISFIED
- ANGRY
- YEAH-NAH
-

Today's stress signals

Breathing

SLOW ○ ○ ○ FAST

Mind

CALM ○ ○ ○ RACING

Concentration

FOCUSED ○ ○ ○ DISTRACTED

Switching off

SIMPLE ○ ○ ○ CHALLENGING

Today's stress danger rating

COOL ← → HOT

Reflect

Stressful moment

Did I 'turn the story around'? How?

Bird's-eye view

Tools I used

- ☐ BREATHE
- ☐ LEAVE
- ☐ MOVE
- ☐ OTHER

Today, I am feeling good about ...

Pause

Did I do my gratitude notes?

◯ YES ◯ NO

Feeling before

Feeling after

Did I take a mindfulness pause?

◯ YES ◯ NO

Feeling before

Feeling after

Pausing improved my stress

FROM /10

TO /10

Connect

3 moments of connection

1.

2.

3.

Person I'm grateful for (and why)

Today's thank you moment

Word of the day

DAY M T W T F S S

DATE / /

Check-in

Today's body feels

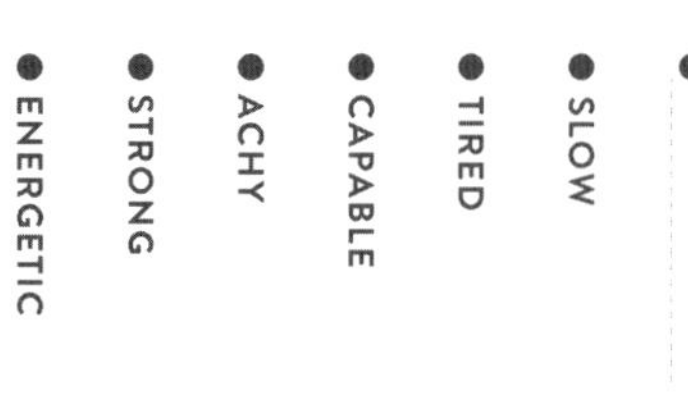

Today's dominant vibe

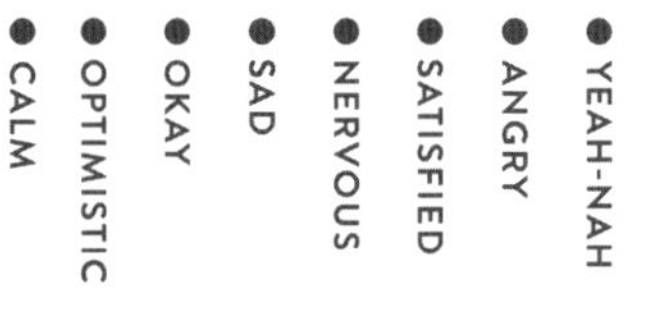

Today's stress signals

Breathing

SLOW ◯ ◯ ◯ FAST

Mind

CALM ◯ ◯ ◯ RACING

Concentration

FOCUSED ◯ ◯ ◯ DISTRACTED

Switching off

SIMPLE ◯ ◯ ◯ CHALLENGING

Today's stress danger rating

COOL ← → HOT

Reflect

Stressful moment

Did I 'turn the story around'? How?

Bird's-eye view

Tools I used

- [ ] BREATHE
- [ ] LEAVE
- [ ] MOVE
- [ ] OTHER

Today, I am feeling good about ...

Pause

Did I do my gratitude notes?

YES NO

Feeling before

Feeling after

Did I take a mindfulness pause?

YES NO

Feeling before

Feeling after

Pausing improved my stress

FROM /10 TO /10

Connect

3 moments of connection

1.

2.

3.

Person I'm grateful for (and why)

Today's thank you moment

Word of the day

DAY M T W T F S S

DATE / /

Check-in

Today's body feels

- ENERGETIC
- STRONG
- ACHY
- CAPABLE
- TIRED
- SLOW
-

Today's dominant vibe

- CALM
- OPTIMISTIC
- OKAY
- SAD
- NERVOUS
- SATISFIED
- ANGRY
- YEAH-NAH
-

Today's stress signals

Breathing

SLOW ○ ○ ○ FAST

Mind

CALM ○ ○ ○ RACING

Concentration

FOCUSED ○ ○ ○ DISTRACTED

Switching off

SIMPLE ○ ○ ○ CHALLENGING

Today's stress danger rating

COOL ← → HOT

Reflect

Stressful moment

Did I 'turn the story around'? How?

Bird's-eye view

Tools I used

- [ ] BREATHE
- [ ] LEAVE
- [ ] MOVE
- [ ] OTHER

Today, I am feeling good about ...

Pause

Did I do my gratitude notes?

◯ YES ◯ NO

Feeling before

Feeling after

Did I take a mindfulness pause?

◯ YES ◯ NO

Feeling before

Feeling after

Pausing improved my stress

FROM /10

TO /10

Connect

3 moments of connection

1.

2.

3.

Person I'm grateful for (and why)

Today's thank you moment

Word of the day

DAY M T W T F S S

DATE / /

Check-in

Today's body feels

ENERGETIC · STRONG · ACHY · CAPABLE · TIRED · SLOW ·

Today's dominant vibe

CALM · OPTIMISTIC · OKAY · SAD · NERVOUS · SATISFIED · ANGRY · YEAH-NAH ·

Today's stress signals

Breathing

SLOW ○ ○ ○ FAST

Mind

CALM ○ ○ ○ RACING

Concentration

FOCUSED ○ ○ ○ DISTRACTED

Switching off

SIMPLE ○ ○ ○ CHALLENGING

Today's stress danger rating

COOL ← → HOT

Reflect

Stressful moment

Did I 'turn the story around'? How?

Bird's-eye view

Tools I used

☐ BREATHE

☐ LEAVE

☐ MOVE

☐ OTHER

Today, I am feeling good about ...

Pause

Did I do my gratitude notes?

YES NO

Feeling before

Feeling after

Did I take a mindfulness pause?

YES NO

Feeling before

Feeling after

Pausing improved my stress

FROM /10

TO /10

Connect

3 moments of connection

1.

2.

3.

Person I'm grateful for (and why)

Today's thank you moment

Word of the day

DAY M T W T F S S

DATE / /

Check-in

Today's body feels

- ENERGETIC
- STRONG
- ACHY
- CAPABLE
- TIRED
- SLOW
-

Today's dominant vibe

- CALM
- OPTIMISTIC
- OKAY
- SAD
- NERVOUS
- SATISFIED
- ANGRY
- YEAH-NAH
-

Today's stress signals

Breathing

SLOW ○ ○ ○ FAST

Mind

CALM ○ ○ ○ RACING

Concentration

FOCUSED ○ ○ ○ DISTRACTED

Switching off

SIMPLE ○ ○ ○ CHALLENGING

Today's stress danger rating

COOL ← → HOT

Reflect

Stressful moment

Did I 'turn the story around'? How?

Bird's-eye view

Tools I used

- ☐ BREATHE
- ☐ LEAVE
- ☐ MOVE
- ☐ OTHER

Today, I am feeling good about ...

Pause

Did I do my gratitude notes?

◯ YES ◯ NO

Feeling before

Feeling after

Did I take a mindfulness pause?

◯ YES ◯ NO

Feeling before

Feeling after

Pausing improved my stress

FROM /10

TO /10

Connect

3 moments of connection

1.

2.

3.

Person I'm grateful for (and why)

Today's thank you moment

Word of the day

DAY M T W T F S S

DATE / /

Check-in

Today's body feels

- ENERGETIC
- STRONG
- ACHY
- CAPABLE
- TIRED
- SLOW
-

Today's dominant vibe

- CALM
- OPTIMISTIC
- OKAY
- SAD
- NERVOUS
- SATISFIED
- ANGRY
- YEAH-NAH
-

Today's stress signals

Breathing

SLOW ○ ○ ○ FAST

Mind

CALM ○ ○ ○ RACING

Concentration

FOCUSED ○ ○ ○ DISTRACTED

Switching off

SIMPLE ○ ○ ○ CHALLENGING

Today's stress danger rating

COOL ← → HOT

Reflect

Stressful moment

Did I 'turn the story around'? How?

Bird's-eye view

Tools I used

- [ ] BREATHE
- [ ] LEAVE
- [ ] MOVE
- [ ] OTHER

Today, I am feeling good about ...

Pause

Did I do my gratitude notes?

YES NO

Feeling before

Feeling after

Did I take a mindfulness pause?

YES NO

Feeling before

Feeling after

Pausing improved my stress

FROM /10

TO /10

Connect

3 moments of connection

1.

2.

3.

Person I'm grateful for (and why)

Today's thank you moment

Word of the day

DAY M T W T F S S

DATE / /

Check-in

Today's body feels

- ENERGETIC
- STRONG
- ACHY
- CAPABLE
- TIRED
- SLOW
-

Today's dominant vibe

- CALM
- OPTIMISTIC
- OKAY
- SAD
- NERVOUS
- SATISFIED
- ANGRY
- YEAH-NAH
-

Today's stress signals

Breathing

SLOW ◯ ◯ ◯ FAST

Mind

CALM ◯ ◯ ◯ RACING

Concentration

FOCUSED ◯ ◯ ◯ DISTRACTED

Switching off

SIMPLE ◯ ◯ ◯ CHALLENGING

Today's stress danger rating

COOL ← → HOT

Reflect

Stressful moment

Did I 'turn the story around'? How?

Bird's-eye view

Tools I used

- [ ] BREATHE
- [ ] LEAVE
- [ ] MOVE
- [ ] OTHER

Today, I am feeling good about ...

Pause

Did I do my gratitude notes?

YES NO

Feeling before

Feeling after

Did I take a mindfulness pause?

YES NO

Feeling before

Feeling after

Pausing improved my stress

FROM /10

TO /10

Connect

3 moments of connection

1.

2.

3.

Person I'm grateful for (and why)

Today's thank you moment

Word of the day

DAY M T W T F S S

DATE / /

Check-in

Today's body feels

- ENERGETIC
- STRONG
- ACHY
- CAPABLE
- TIRED
- SLOW

Today's dominant vibe

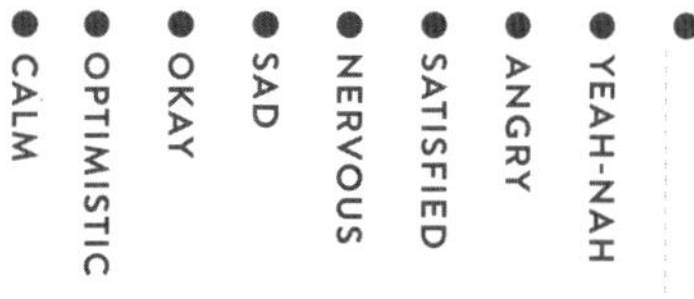

- CALM
- OPTIMISTIC
- OKAY
- SAD
- NERVOUS
- SATISFIED
- ANGRY
- YEAH-NAH

Today's stress signals

Breathing

SLOW ○ ○ ○ FAST

Mind

CALM ○ ○ ○ RACING

Concentration

FOCUSED ○ ○ ○ DISTRACTED

Switching off

SIMPLE ○ ○ ○ CHALLENGING

Today's stress danger rating

COOL ← → HOT

Reflect

Stressful moment

Did I 'turn the story around'? How?

Bird's-eye view

Tools I used

- ☐ BREATHE
- ☐ LEAVE
- ☐ MOVE
- ☐ OTHER

Today, I am feeling good about ...

Pause

Did I do my gratitude notes?

◯ YES ◯ NO

Feeling before

Feeling after

Did I take a mindfulness pause?

◯ YES ◯ NO

Feeling before

Feeling after

Pausing improved my stress

FROM /10

TO /10

Connect

3 moments of connection

1.

2.

3.

Person I'm grateful for (and why)

Today's thank you moment

Word of the day

DAY M T W T F S S

DATE / /

Check-in

Today's body feels

- ENERGETIC
- STRONG
- ACHY
- CAPABLE
- TIRED
- SLOW

Today's dominant vibe

- CALM
- OPTIMISTIC
- OKAY
- SAD
- NERVOUS
- SATISFIED
- ANGRY
- YEAH-NAH

Today's stress signals

Breathing

SLOW ○ ○ ○ FAST

Mind

CALM ○ ○ ○ RACING

Concentration

FOCUSED ○ ○ ○ DISTRACTED

Switching off

SIMPLE ○ ○ ○ CHALLENGING

Today's stress danger rating

COOL ← → HOT

Reflect

Stressful moment

Did I 'turn the story around'? How?

Bird's-eye view

Tools I used

- ☐ BREATHE
- ☐ LEAVE
- ☐ MOVE
- ☐ OTHER

Today, I am feeling good about ...

Pause

Did I do my gratitude notes?

◯ YES ◯ NO

Feeling before

Feeling after

Did I take a mindfulness pause?

◯ YES ◯ NO

Feeling before

Feeling after

Pausing improved my stress

FROM /10 TO /10

Connect

3 moments of connection

1.

2.

3.

Person I'm grateful for (and why)

Today's thank you moment

Word of the day

DAY M T W T F S S

DATE / /

Check-in

Today's body feels

- ENERGETIC
- STRONG
- ACHY
- CAPABLE
- TIRED
- SLOW
-

Today's dominant vibe

- CALM
- OPTIMISTIC
- OKAY
- SAD
- NERVOUS
- SATISFIED
- ANGRY
- YEAH-NAH
-

Today's stress signals

Breathing

SLOW ○ ○ ○ FAST

Mind

CALM ○ ○ ○ RACING

Concentration

FOCUSED ○ ○ ○ DISTRACTED

Switching off

SIMPLE ○ ○ ○ CHALLENGING

Today's stress danger rating

COOL ← → HOT

Reflect

Stressful moment

Did I 'turn the story around'? How?

Bird's-eye view

Tools I used

- ☐ BREATHE
- ☐ LEAVE
- ☐ MOVE
- ☐ OTHER

Today, I am feeling good about ...

Pause

Did I do my gratitude notes?

YES NO

Feeling before

Feeling after

Did I take a mindfulness pause?

YES NO

Feeling before

Feeling after

Pausing improved my stress

FROM /10 TO /10

Connect

3 moments of connection

1.

2.

3.

Person I'm grateful for (and why)

Today's thank you moment

Word of the day

DAY M T W T F S S

DATE / /

Check-in

Today's body feels

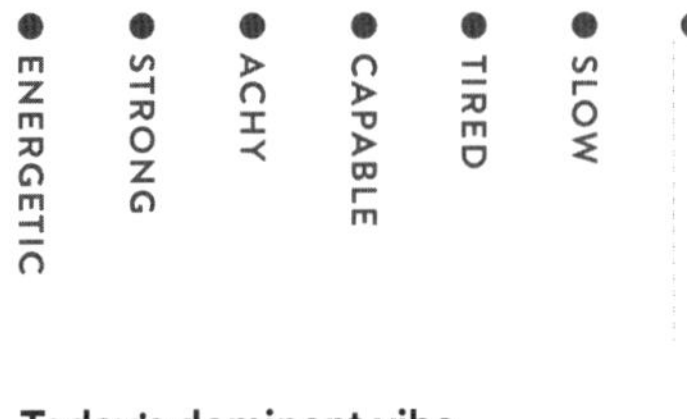

Today's dominant vibe

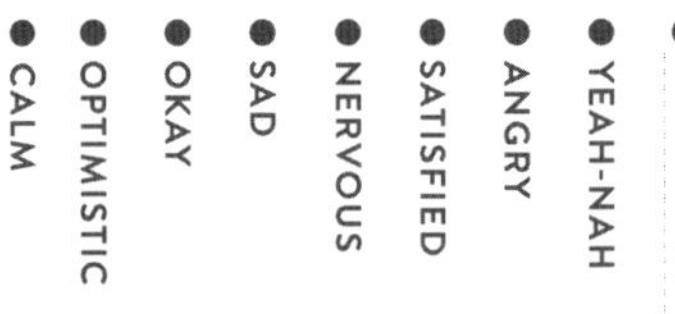

Today's stress signals

Breathing

SLOW ○ ○ ○ FAST

Mind

CALM ○ ○ ○ RACING

Concentration

FOCUSED ○ ○ ○ DISTRACTED

Switching off

SIMPLE ○ ○ ○ CHALLENGING

Today's stress danger rating

COOL ← → HOT

Reflect

Stressful moment

Did I 'turn the story around'? How?

Bird's-eye view

Tools I used

- [ ] BREATHE
- [ ] LEAVE
- [ ] MOVE
- [ ] OTHER

Today, I am feeling good about ...

Pause

Did I do my gratitude notes?

◯ YES ◯ NO

Feeling before

Feeling after

Did I take a mindfulness pause?

◯ YES ◯ NO

Feeling before

Feeling after

Pausing improved my stress

FROM /10

TO /10

Connect

3 moments of connection

1.

2.

3.

Person I'm grateful for (and why)

Today's thank you moment

Word of the day

DAY M T W T F S S

DATE / /

Check-in

Today's body feels

- ENERGETIC
- STRONG
- ACHY
- CAPABLE
- TIRED
- SLOW

Today's dominant vibe

- CALM
- OPTIMISTIC
- OKAY
- SAD
- NERVOUS
- SATISFIED
- ANGRY
- YEAH-NAH

Today's stress signals

Breathing

SLOW ○ ○ ○ FAST

Mind

CALM ○ ○ ○ RACING

Concentration

FOCUSED ○ ○ ○ DISTRACTED

Switching off

SIMPLE ○ ○ ○ CHALLENGING

Today's stress danger rating

COOL ← → HOT

Reflect

Stressful moment

Did I 'turn the story around'? How?

Bird's-eye view

Tools I used

- ☐ BREATHE
- ☐ LEAVE
- ☐ MOVE
- ☐ OTHER

Today, I am feeling good about ...

Pause

Did I do my gratitude notes?

◯ YES ◯ NO

Feeling before

Feeling after

Did I take a mindfulness pause?

◯ YES ◯ NO

Feeling before

Feeling after

Pausing improved my stress

FROM /10

TO /10

Connect

3 moments of connection

1.

2.

3.

Person I'm grateful for (and why)

Today's thank you moment

Word of the day

DAY M T W T F S S

DATE / /

Check-in

Today's body feels

- ENERGETIC
- STRONG
- ACHY
- CAPABLE
- TIRED
- SLOW
-

Today's dominant vibe

- CALM
- OPTIMISTIC
- OKAY
- SAD
- NERVOUS
- SATISFIED
- ANGRY
- YEAH-NAH
-

Today's stress signals

Breathing

SLOW ○ ○ ○ FAST

Mind

CALM ○ ○ ○ RACING

Concentration

FOCUSED ○ ○ ○ DISTRACTED

Switching off

SIMPLE ○ ○ ○ CHALLENGING

Today's stress danger rating

COOL ← → HOT

Reflect

Stressful moment

Did I 'turn the story around'? How?

Bird's-eye view

Tools I used

- ☐ BREATHE
- ☐ LEAVE
- ☐ MOVE
- ☐ OTHER

Today, I am feeling good about ...

Pause

Did I do my gratitude notes?

YES NO

Feeling before

Feeling after

Did I take a mindfulness pause?

YES NO

Feeling before

Feeling after

Pausing improved my stress

FROM /10

TO /10

Connect

3 moments of connection

1.

2.

3.

Person I'm grateful for (and why)

Today's thank you moment

Word of the day

DAY M T W T F S S

DATE / /

Check-in

Today's body feels

- ENERGETIC
- STRONG
- ACHY
- CAPABLE
- TIRED
- SLOW
-

Today's dominant vibe

- CALM
- OPTIMISTIC
- OKAY
- SAD
- NERVOUS
- SATISFIED
- ANGRY
- YEAH-NAH
-

Today's stress signals

Breathing

SLOW ◯ ◯ ◯ FAST

Mind

CALM ◯ ◯ ◯ RACING

Concentration

FOCUSED ◯ ◯ ◯ DISTRACTED

Switching off

SIMPLE ◯ ◯ ◯ CHALLENGING

Today's stress danger rating

COOL ← → HOT

Reflect

Stressful moment

Did I 'turn the story around'? How?

Bird's-eye view

Tools I used

- ☐ BREATHE
- ☐ LEAVE
- ☐ MOVE
- ☐ OTHER

Today, I am feeling good about ...

Pause

Did I do my gratitude notes?

◯ YES ◯ NO

Feeling before

Feeling after

Did I take a mindfulness pause?

◯ YES ◯ NO

Feeling before

Feeling after

Pausing improved my stress

FROM /10 TO /10

Connect

3 moments of connection

1.

2.

3.

Person I'm grateful for (and why)

Today's thank you moment

Word of the day

DAY M T W T F S S

DATE / /

Check-in

Today's body feels

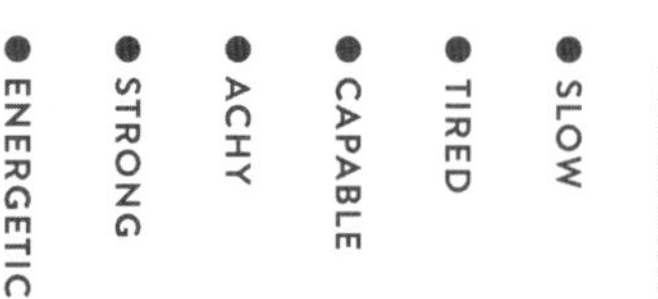

Today's dominant vibe

CALM

OPTIMISTIC

OKAY

SAD

NERVOUS

SATISFIED

ANGRY

YEAH-NAH

Today's stress signals

Breathing

SLOW ○ ○ ○ FAST

Mind

CALM ○ ○ ○ RACING

Concentration

FOCUSED ○ ○ ○ DISTRACTED

Switching off

SIMPLE ○ ○ ○ CHALLENGING

Today's stress danger rating

COOL ← → HOT

Reflect

Stressful moment

Did I 'turn the story around'? How?

Bird's-eye view

Tools I used

- [ ] BREATHE
- [ ] LEAVE
- [ ] MOVE
- [ ] OTHER

Today, I am feeling good about ...

Pause

Did I do my gratitude notes?

YES NO

Feeling before

Feeling after

Did I take a mindfulness pause?

YES NO

Feeling before

Feeling after

Pausing improved my stress

FROM /10 TO /10

Connect

3 moments of connection

1.

2.

3.

Person I'm grateful for (and why)

Today's thank you moment

Word of the day

DAY M T W T F S S

DATE / /

Check-in

Today's body feels

- ENERGETIC
- STRONG
- ACHY
- CAPABLE
- TIRED
- SLOW
-

Today's dominant vibe

- CALM
- OPTIMISTIC
- OKAY
- SAD
- NERVOUS
- SATISFIED
- ANGRY
- YEAH-NAH
-

Today's stress signals

Breathing

SLOW ○ ○ ○ FAST

Mind

CALM ○ ○ ○ RACING

Concentration

FOCUSED ○ ○ ○ DISTRACTED

Switching off

SIMPLE ○ ○ ○ CHALLENGING

Today's stress danger rating

COOL ← → HOT

Reflect

Stressful moment

Did I 'turn the story around'? How?

Bird's-eye view

Tools I used

- ☐ BREATHE
- ☐ LEAVE
- ☐ MOVE
- ☐ OTHER

Today, I am feeling good about ...

Pause

Did I do my gratitude notes?

◯ YES ◯ NO

Feeling before

Feeling after

Did I take a mindfulness pause?

◯ YES ◯ NO

Feeling before

Feeling after

Pausing improved my stress

FROM /10 TO /10

Connect

3 moments of connection

1.

2.

3.

Person I'm grateful for (and why)

Today's thank you moment

Word of the day

DAY M T W T F S S

DATE / /

Check-in

Today's body feels

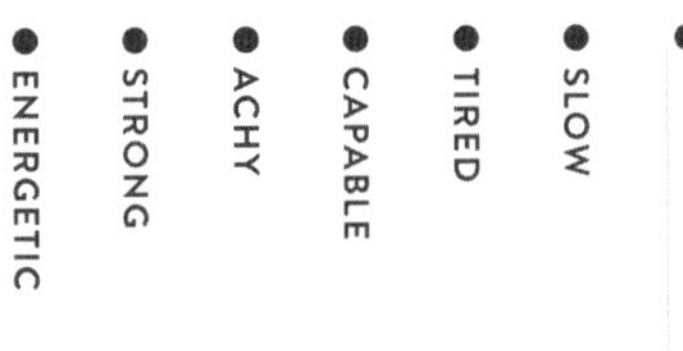

Today's dominant vibe

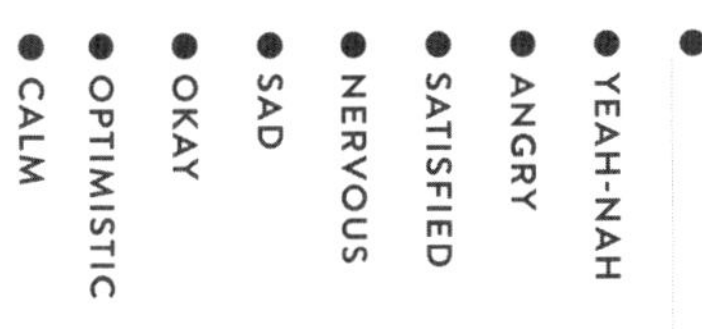

Today's stress signals

Breathing

SLOW ○ ○ ○ FAST

Mind

CALM ○ ○ ○ RACING

Concentration

FOCUSED ○ ○ ○ DISTRACTED

Switching off

SIMPLE ○ ○ ○ CHALLENGING

Today's stress danger rating

COOL ← → HOT

Reflect

Stressful moment

Did I 'turn the story around'? How?

Bird's-eye view

Tools I used

☐ BREATHE

☐ LEAVE

☐ MOVE

☐ OTHER

Today, I am feeling good about ...

Pause

Did I do my gratitude notes?

YES NO

Feeling before

Feeling after

Did I take a mindfulness pause?

YES NO

Feeling before

Feeling after

Pausing improved my stress

FROM /10 TO /10

Connect

3 moments of connection

1.

2.

3.

Person I'm grateful for (and why)

Today's thank you moment

Word of the day

DAY M T W T F S S

DATE / /

Check-in

Today's body feels

- ENERGETIC
- STRONG
- ACHY
- CAPABLE
- TIRED
- SLOW
-

Today's dominant vibe

- CALM
- OPTIMISTIC
- OKAY
- SAD
- NERVOUS
- SATISFIED
- ANGRY
- YEAH-NAH
-

Today's stress signals

Breathing

SLOW ○ ○ ○ FAST

Mind

CALM ○ ○ ○ RACING

Concentration

FOCUSED ○ ○ ○ DISTRACTED

Switching off

SIMPLE ○ ○ ○ CHALLENGING

Today's stress danger rating

COOL ← → HOT

Reflect

Stressful moment

Did I 'turn the story around'? How?

Bird's-eye view

Tools I used

- ☐ BREATHE
- ☐ LEAVE
- ☐ MOVE
- ☐ OTHER

Today, I am feeling good about ...

Pause

Did I do my gratitude notes?

YES NO

Feeling before

Feeling after

Did I take a mindfulness pause?

YES NO

Feeling before

Feeling after

Pausing improved my stress

FROM /10

TO /10

Connect

3 moments of connection

1.

2.

3.

Person I'm grateful for (and why)

Today's thank you moment

Word of the day

DAY M T W T F S S

DATE / /

Check-in

Today's body feels

- ENERGETIC
- STRONG
- ACHY
- CAPABLE
- TIRED
- SLOW
-

Today's dominant vibe

- CALM
- OPTIMISTIC
- OKAY
- SAD
- NERVOUS
- SATISFIED
- ANGRY
- YEAH-NAH
-

Today's stress signals

Breathing

SLOW ○ ○ ○ FAST

Mind

CALM ○ ○ ○ RACING

Concentration

FOCUSED ○ ○ ○ DISTRACTED

Switching off

SIMPLE ○ ○ ○ CHALLENGING

Today's stress danger rating

COOL ← → HOT

Reflect

Stressful moment

Did I 'turn the story around'? How?

Bird's-eye view

Tools I used

- ☐ BREATHE
- ☐ LEAVE
- ☐ MOVE
- ☐ OTHER

Today, I am feeling good about ...

Pause

Did I do my gratitude notes?

◯ YES ◯ NO

Feeling before

Feeling after

Did I take a mindfulness pause?

◯ YES ◯ NO

Feeling before

Feeling after

Pausing improved my stress

FROM /10 TO /10

Connect

3 moments of connection

1.

2.

3.

Person I'm grateful for (and why)

Today's thank you moment

Word of the day

DAY M T W T F S S

DATE / /

Check-in

Today's body feels

- ENERGETIC
- STRONG
- ACHY
- CAPABLE
- TIRED
- SLOW

Today's dominant vibe

- CALM
- OPTIMISTIC
- OKAY
- SAD
- NERVOUS
- SATISFIED
- ANGRY
- YEAH-NAH

Today's stress signals

Breathing

SLOW ○ ○ ○ FAST

Mind

CALM ○ ○ ○ RACING

Concentration

FOCUSED ○ ○ ○ DISTRACTED

Switching off

SIMPLE ○ ○ ○ CHALLENGING

Today's stress danger rating

COOL ← → HOT

Reflect

Stressful moment

Did I 'turn the story around'? How?

Bird's-eye view

Tools I used

- ☐ BREATHE
- ☐ LEAVE
- ☐ MOVE
- ☐ OTHER

Today, I am feeling good about ...

Pause

Did I do my gratitude notes?

◯ YES ◯ NO

Feeling before

Feeling after

Did I take a mindfulness pause?

◯ YES ◯ NO

Feeling before

Feeling after

Pausing improved my stress

FROM /10 TO /10

Connect

3 moments of connection

1.

2.

3.

Person I'm grateful for (and why)

Today's thank you moment

Word of the day

DAY M T W T F S S

DATE / /

Check-in

Today's body feels

- ENERGETIC
- STRONG
- ACHY
- CAPABLE
- TIRED
- SLOW
-

Today's dominant vibe

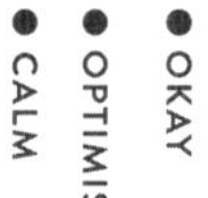

- CALM
- OPTIMISTIC
- OKAY
- SAD
- NERVOUS
- SATISFIED
- ANGRY
- YEAH-NAH
-

Today's stress signals

Breathing

SLOW ○ ○ ○ FAST

Mind

CALM ○ ○ ○ RACING

Concentration

FOCUSED ○ ○ ○ DISTRACTED

Switching off

SIMPLE ○ ○ ○ CHALLENGING

Today's stress danger rating

COOL ← → HOT

Reflect

Stressful moment

Did I 'turn the story around'? How?

Bird's-eye view

Tools I used

- ☐ BREATHE
- ☐ LEAVE
- ☐ MOVE
- ☐ OTHER

Today, I am feeling good about ...

Pause

Did I do my gratitude notes?

YES NO

Feeling before

Feeling after

Did I take a mindfulness pause?

YES NO

Feeling before

Feeling after

Pausing improved my stress

FROM /10 TO /10

Connect

3 moments of connection

1.

2.

3.

Person I'm grateful for (and why)

Today's thank you moment

Word of the day

DAY M T W T F S S

DATE / /

Check-in

Today's body feels

- ENERGETIC
- STRONG
- ACHY
- CAPABLE
- TIRED
- SLOW
-

Today's dominant vibe

- CALM
- OPTIMISTIC
- OKAY
- SAD
- NERVOUS
- SATISFIED
- ANGRY
- YEAH-NAH
-

Today's stress signals

Breathing

SLOW ○ ○ ○ FAST

Mind

CALM ○ ○ ○ RACING

Concentration

FOCUSED ○ ○ ○ DISTRACTED

Switching off

SIMPLE ○ ○ ○ CHALLENGING

Today's stress danger rating

COOL ← → HOT

Reflect

Stressful moment

Did I 'turn the story around'? How?

Bird's-eye view

Tools I used

- [ ] BREATHE
- [ ] LEAVE
- [ ] MOVE
- [ ] OTHER

Today, I am feeling good about ...

Pause

Did I do my gratitude notes?

YES NO

Feeling before

Feeling after

Did I take a mindfulness pause?

YES NO

Feeling before

Feeling after

Pausing improved my stress

FROM /10

TO /10

Connect

3 moments of connection

1.

2.

3.

Person I'm grateful for (and why)

Today's thank you moment

Word of the day

DAY M T W T F S S

DATE / /

Check-in

Today's body feels

- ENERGETIC
- STRONG
- ACHY
- CAPABLE
- TIRED
- SLOW
-

Today's dominant vibe

- CALM
- OPTIMISTIC
- OKAY
- SAD
- NERVOUS
- SATISFIED
- ANGRY
- YEAH-NAH
-

Today's stress signals

Breathing

SLOW ○ ○ ○ FAST

Mind

CALM ○ ○ ○ RACING

Concentration

FOCUSED ○ ○ ○ DISTRACTED

Switching off

SIMPLE ○ ○ ○ CHALLENGING

Today's stress danger rating

COOL ← → HOT

Reflect

Stressful moment

Did I 'turn the story around'? How?

Bird's-eye view

Tools I used

- ☐ BREATHE
- ☐ LEAVE
- ☐ MOVE
- ☐ OTHER

Today, I am feeling good about ...

Pause

Did I do my gratitude notes?

YES NO

Feeling before

Feeling after

Did I take a mindfulness pause?

YES NO

Feeling before

Feeling after

Pausing improved my stress

FROM /10

TO /10

Connect

3 moments of connection

1.

2.

3.

Person I'm grateful for (and why)

Today's thank you moment

Word of the day

DAY M T W T F S S

DATE / /

Check-in

Today's body feels

- ENERGETIC
- STRONG
- ACHY
- CAPABLE
- TIRED
- SLOW

Today's dominant vibe

- CALM
- OPTIMISTIC
- OKAY
- SAD
- NERVOUS
- SATISFIED
- ANGRY
- YEAH-NAH

Today's stress signals

Breathing

SLOW ○ ○ ○ FAST

Mind

CALM ○ ○ ○ RACING

Concentration

FOCUSED ○ ○ ○ DISTRACTED

Switching off

SIMPLE ○ ○ ○ CHALLENGING

Today's stress danger rating

COOL ← → HOT

Reflect

Stressful moment

Did I 'turn the story around'? How?

Bird's-eye view

Tools I used

- [ ] BREATHE
- [ ] LEAVE
- [ ] MOVE
- [ ] OTHER

Today, I am feeling good about ...

Pause

Did I do my gratitude notes?

◯ YES ◯ NO

Feeling before

Feeling after

Did I take a mindfulness pause?

◯ YES ◯ NO

Feeling before

Feeling after

Pausing improved my stress

FROM /10

TO /10

Connect

3 moments of connection

1.

2.

3.

Person I'm grateful for (and why)

Today's thank you moment

Word of the day

DAY M T W T F S S

DATE / /

Check-in

Today's body feels

- ENERGETIC
- STRONG
- ACHY
- CAPABLE
- TIRED
- SLOW
-

Today's dominant vibe

- CALM
- OPTIMISTIC
- OKAY
- SAD
- NERVOUS
- SATISFIED
- ANGRY
- YEAH-NAH
-

Today's stress signals

Breathing

SLOW ○ ○ ○ FAST

Mind

CALM ○ ○ ○ RACING

Concentration

FOCUSED ○ ○ ○ DISTRACTED

Switching off

SIMPLE ○ ○ ○ CHALLENGING

Today's stress danger rating

COOL ← → HOT

Reflect

Stressful moment

Did I 'turn the story around'? How?

Bird's-eye view

Tools I used

- ☐ BREATHE
- ☐ LEAVE
- ☐ MOVE
- ☐ OTHER

Today, I am feeling good about ...

Pause

Did I do my gratitude notes?

◯ YES ◯ NO

Feeling before

Feeling after

Did I take a mindfulness pause?

◯ YES ◯ NO

Feeling before

Feeling after

Pausing improved my stress

FROM /10 TO /10

Connect

3 moments of connection

1.

2.

3.

Person I'm grateful for (and why)

Today's thank you moment

Word of the day

DAY M T W T F S S

DATE / /

Check-in

Today's body feels

- ENERGETIC
- STRONG
- ACHY
- CAPABLE
- TIRED
- SLOW

Today's dominant vibe

- CALM
- OPTIMISTIC
- OKAY
- SAD
- NERVOUS
- SATISFIED
- ANGRY
- YEAH-NAH

Today's stress signals

Breathing

SLOW ○ ○ ○ FAST

Mind

CALM ○ ○ ○ RACING

Concentration

FOCUSED ○ ○ ○ DISTRACTED

Switching off

SIMPLE ○ ○ ○ CHALLENGING

Today's stress danger rating

COOL ← → HOT

Reflect

Stressful moment

Did I 'turn the story around'? How?

Bird's-eye view

Tools I used

- ☐ BREATHE
- ☐ LEAVE
- ☐ MOVE
- ☐ OTHER

Today, I am feeling good about ...

Pause

Did I do my gratitude notes?

○ YES ○ NO

Feeling before

Feeling after

Did I take a mindfulness pause?

○ YES ○ NO

Feeling before

Feeling after

Pausing improved my stress

FROM /10 TO /10

Connect

3 moments of connection

1.

2.

3.

Person I'm grateful for (and why)

Today's thank you moment

Word of the day

DAY M T W T F S S

DATE / /

Check-in

Today's body feels

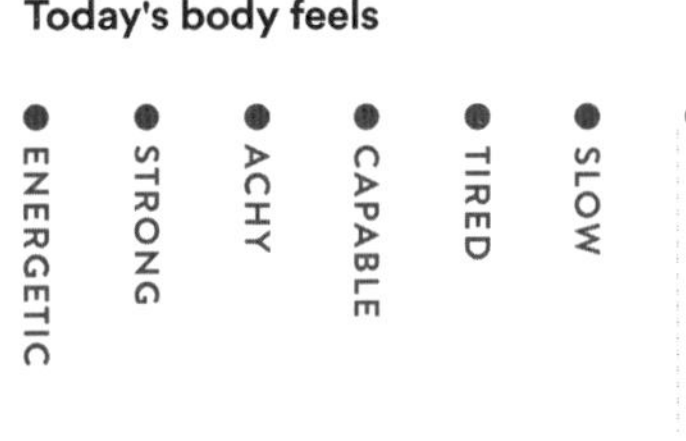

Today's dominant vibe

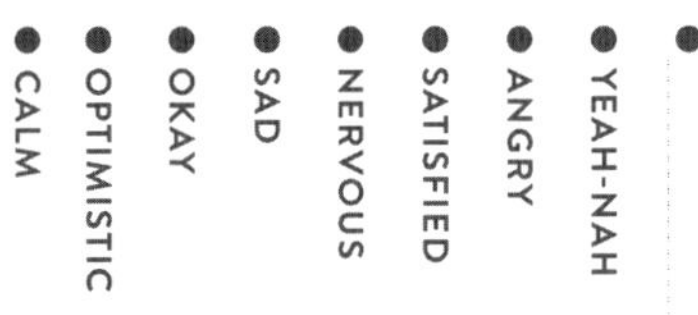

Today's stress signals

Breathing

SLOW ○ ○ ○ FAST

Mind

CALM ○ ○ ○ RACING

Concentration

FOCUSED ○ ○ ○ DISTRACTED

Switching off

SIMPLE ○ ○ ○ CHALLENGING

Today's stress danger rating

COOL ← → HOT

Reflect

Stressful moment

Did I 'turn the story around'? How?

Bird's-eye view

Tools I used

☐ BREATHE

☐ LEAVE

☐ MOVE

☐ OTHER

Today, I am feeling good about ...

Pause

Did I do my gratitude notes?

◯ YES ◯ NO

Feeling before

Feeling after

Did I take a mindfulness pause?

◯ YES ◯ NO

Feeling before

Feeling after

Pausing improved my stress

FROM /10 TO /10

Connect

3 moments of connection

1.

2.

3.

Person I'm grateful for (and why)

Today's thank you moment

Word of the day

DAY M T W T F S S

DATE / /

Check-in

Today's body feels

- ENERGETIC
- STRONG
- ACHY
- CAPABLE
- TIRED
- SLOW

Today's dominant vibe

- CALM
- OPTIMISTIC
- OKAY
- SAD
- NERVOUS
- SATISFIED
- ANGRY
- YEAH-NAH

Today's stress signals

Breathing

SLOW ◯ ◯ ◯ FAST

Mind

CALM ◯ ◯ ◯ RACING

Concentration

FOCUSED ◯ ◯ ◯ DISTRACTED

Switching off

SIMPLE ◯ ◯ ◯ CHALLENGING

Today's stress danger rating

COOL ← → HOT

Reflect

Stressful moment

Did I 'turn the story around'? How?

Bird's-eye view

Tools I used

- ☐ BREATHE
- ☐ LEAVE
- ☐ MOVE
- ☐ OTHER

Today, I am feeling good about ...

Pause

Did I do my gratitude notes?

○ YES ○ NO

Feeling before

Feeling after

Did I take a mindfulness pause?

○ YES ○ NO

Feeling before

Feeling after

Pausing improved my stress

FROM /10

TO /10

Connect

3 moments of connection

1.

2.

3.

Person I'm grateful for (and why)

Today's thank you moment

Word of the day

DAY M T W T F S S

DATE / /

Check-in

Today's body feels

- ENERGETIC
- STRONG
- ACHY
- CAPABLE
- TIRED
- SLOW
-

Today's dominant vibe

- CALM
- OPTIMISTIC
- OKAY
- SAD
- NERVOUS
- SATISFIED
- ANGRY
- YEAH-NAH
-

Today's stress signals

Breathing

SLOW ◯ ◯ ◯ FAST

Mind

CALM ◯ ◯ ◯ RACING

Concentration

FOCUSED ◯ ◯ ◯ DISTRACTED

Switching off

SIMPLE ◯ ◯ ◯ CHALLENGING

Today's stress danger rating

COOL ← → HOT

Reflect

Stressful moment

Did I 'turn the story around'? How?

Bird's-eye view

Tools I used

- ☐ BREATHE
- ☐ LEAVE
- ☐ MOVE
- ☐ OTHER

Today, I am feeling good about ...

Pause

Did I do my gratitude notes?

◯ YES ◯ NO

Feeling before

Feeling after

Did I take a mindfulness pause?

◯ YES ◯ NO

Feeling before

Feeling after

Pausing improved my stress

FROM /10 TO /10

Connect

3 moments of connection

1.

2.

3.

Person I'm grateful for (and why)

Today's thank you moment

Word of the day

DAY M T W T F S S

DATE / /

Check-in

Today's body feels

- ENERGETIC
- STRONG
- ACHY
- CAPABLE
- TIRED
- SLOW
-

Today's dominant vibe

- CALM
- OPTIMISTIC
- OKAY
- SAD
- NERVOUS
- SATISFIED
- ANGRY
- YEAH-NAH
-

Today's stress signals

Breathing

SLOW ○ ○ ○ FAST

Mind

CALM ○ ○ ○ RACING

Concentration

FOCUSED ○ ○ ○ DISTRACTED

Switching off

SIMPLE ○ ○ ○ CHALLENGING

Today's stress danger rating

COOL ← → HOT

Reflect

Stressful moment

Did I 'turn the story around'? How?

Bird's-eye view

Tools I used

- ☐ BREATHE
- ☐ LEAVE
- ☐ MOVE
- ☐ OTHER

Today, I am feeling good about ...

Pause

Did I do my gratitude notes?

◯ YES ◯ NO

Feeling before

Feeling after

Did I take a mindfulness pause?

◯ YES ◯ NO

Feeling before

Feeling after

Pausing improved my stress

FROM /10 TO /10

Connect

3 moments of connection

1.

2.

3.

Person I'm grateful for (and why)

Today's thank you moment

Word of the day

DAY M T W T F S S

DATE / /

Check-in

Today's body feels

- ENERGETIC
- STRONG
- ACHY
- CAPABLE
- TIRED
- SLOW
-

Today's dominant vibe

- CALM
- OPTIMISTIC
- OKAY
- SAD
- NERVOUS
- SATISFIED
- ANGRY
- YEAH-NAH
-

Today's stress signals

Breathing

SLOW ○ ○ ○ FAST

Mind

CALM ○ ○ ○ RACING

Concentration

FOCUSED ○ ○ ○ DISTRACTED

Switching off

SIMPLE ○ ○ ○ CHALLENGING

Today's stress danger rating

COOL ← → HOT

Reflect

Stressful moment

Did I 'turn the story around'? How?

Bird's-eye view

Tools I used

- ☐ BREATHE
- ☐ LEAVE
- ☐ MOVE
- ☐ OTHER

Today, I am feeling good about ...

Pause

Did I do my gratitude notes?

- YES
- NO

Feeling before

Feeling after

Did I take a mindfulness pause?

- YES
- NO

Feeling before

Feeling after

Pausing improved my stress

FROM /10

TO /10

Connect

3 moments of connection

1.

2.

3.

Person I'm grateful for (and why)

Today's thank you moment

Word of the day

DAY M T W T F S S

DATE / /

Check-in

Today's body feels

- ENERGETIC
- STRONG
- ACHY
- CAPABLE
- TIRED
- SLOW
-

Today's dominant vibe

- CALM
- OPTIMISTIC
- OKAY
- SAD
- NERVOUS
- SATISFIED
- ANGRY
- YEAH-NAH
-

Today's stress signals

Breathing

SLOW ○ ○ ○ FAST

Mind

CALM ○ ○ ○ RACING

Concentration

FOCUSED ○ ○ ○ DISTRACTED

Switching off

SIMPLE ○ ○ ○ CHALLENGING

Today's stress danger rating

COOL ← → HOT

Reflect

Stressful moment

Did I 'turn the story around'? How?

Bird's-eye view

Tools I used

- ☐ BREATHE
- ☐ LEAVE
- ☐ MOVE
- ☐ OTHER

Today, I am feeling good about ...

Pause

Did I do my gratitude notes?

◯ YES ◯ NO

Feeling before

Feeling after

Did I take a mindfulness pause?

◯ YES ◯ NO

Feeling before

Feeling after

Pausing improved my stress

FROM /10

TO /10

Connect

3 moments of connection

1.

2.

3.

Person I'm grateful for (and why)

Today's thank you moment

Word of the day

DAY M T W T F S S

DATE / /

Check-in

Today's body feels

- ENERGETIC
- STRONG
- ACHY
- CAPABLE
- TIRED
- SLOW
-

Today's dominant vibe

- CALM
- OPTIMISTIC
- OKAY
- SAD
- NERVOUS
- SATISFIED
- ANGRY
- YEAH-NAH
-

Today's stress signals

Breathing

SLOW ○ ○ ○ FAST

Mind

CALM ○ ○ ○ RACING

Concentration

FOCUSED ○ ○ ○ DISTRACTED

Switching off

SIMPLE ○ ○ ○ CHALLENGING

Today's stress danger rating

COOL ← → HOT

Reflect

Stressful moment

Did I 'turn the story around'? How?

Bird's-eye view

Tools I used

- ☐ BREATHE
- ☐ LEAVE
- ☐ MOVE
- ☐ OTHER

Today, I am feeling good about ...

Pause

Did I do my gratitude notes?

◯ YES ◯ NO

Feeling before

Feeling after

Did I take a mindfulness pause?

◯ YES ◯ NO

Feeling before

Feeling after

Pausing improved my stress

FROM /10 TO /10

Connect

3 moments of connection

1.

2.

3.

Person I'm grateful for (and why)

Today's thank you moment

Word of the day

DAY M T W T F S S

DATE / /

Check-in

Today's body feels

- ENERGETIC
- STRONG
- ACHY
- CAPABLE
- TIRED
- SLOW
-

Today's dominant vibe

- CALM
- OPTIMISTIC
- OKAY
- SAD
- NERVOUS
- SATISFIED
- ANGRY
- YEAH-NAH
-

Today's stress signals

Breathing

SLOW ○ ○ ○ FAST

Mind

CALM ○ ○ ○ RACING

Concentration

FOCUSED ○ ○ ○ DISTRACTED

Switching off

SIMPLE ○ ○ ○ CHALLENGING

Today's stress danger rating

COOL ← → HOT

Reflect

Stressful moment

Did I 'turn the story around'? How?

Bird's-eye view

Tools I used

- ☐ BREATHE
- ☐ LEAVE
- ☐ MOVE
- ☐ OTHER

Today, I am feeling good about ...

Pause

Did I do my gratitude notes?

◯ YES ◯ NO

Feeling before

Feeling after

Did I take a mindfulness pause?

◯ YES ◯ NO

Feeling before

Feeling after

Pausing improved my stress

FROM /10 TO /10

Connect

3 moments of connection

1.

2.

3.

Person I'm grateful for (and why)

Today's thank you moment

Word of the day

DAY M T W T F S S

DATE / /

Check-in

Today's body feels

- ENERGETIC
- STRONG
- ACHY
- CAPABLE
- TIRED
- SLOW
-

Today's dominant vibe

- CALM
- OPTIMISTIC
- OKAY
- SAD
- NERVOUS
- SATISFIED
- ANGRY
- YEAH-NAH
-

Today's stress signals

Breathing

SLOW ○ ○ ○ FAST

Mind

CALM ○ ○ ○ RACING

Concentration

FOCUSED ○ ○ ○ DISTRACTED

Switching off

SIMPLE ○ ○ ○ CHALLENGING

Today's stress danger rating

COOL ← → HOT

Reflect

Stressful moment

Did I 'turn the story around'? How?

Bird's-eye view

Tools I used

☐ BREATHE

☐ LEAVE

☐ MOVE

☐ OTHER

Today, I am feeling good about ...

Pause

Did I do my gratitude notes?

◯ YES ◯ NO

Feeling before

Feeling after

Did I take a mindfulness pause?

◯ YES ◯ NO

Feeling before

Feeling after

Pausing improved my stress

FROM /10

TO /10

Connect

3 moments of connection

1.

2.

3.

Person I'm grateful for (and why)

Today's thank you moment

Word of the day

DAY M T W T F S S

DATE / /

Check-in

Today's body feels

- ENERGETIC
- STRONG
- ACHY
- CAPABLE
- TIRED
- SLOW
-

Today's dominant vibe

- CALM
- OPTIMISTIC
- OKAY
- SAD
- NERVOUS
- SATISFIED
- ANGRY
- YEAH-NAH
-

Today's stress signals

Breathing

SLOW ○ ○ ○ FAST

Mind

CALM ○ ○ ○ RACING

Concentration

FOCUSED ○ ○ ○ DISTRACTED

Switching off

SIMPLE ○ ○ ○ CHALLENGING

Today's stress danger rating

COOL ← → HOT

Reflect

Stressful moment

Did I 'turn the story around'? How?

Bird's-eye view

Tools I used

- ☐ BREATHE
- ☐ LEAVE
- ☐ MOVE
- ☐ OTHER

Today, I am feeling good about ...

Pause

Did I do my gratitude notes?

YES NO

Feeling before

Feeling after

Did I take a mindfulness pause?

YES NO

Feeling before

Feeling after

Pausing improved my stress

FROM /10 TO /10

Connect

3 moments of connection

1.

2.

3.

Person I'm grateful for (and why)

Today's thank you moment

Word of the day

DAY M T W T F S S

DATE / /

Check-in

Today's body feels

- ENERGETIC
- STRONG
- ACHY
- CAPABLE
- TIRED
- SLOW
-

Today's dominant vibe

- CALM
- OPTIMISTIC
- OKAY
- SAD
- NERVOUS
- SATISFIED
- ANGRY
- YEAH-NAH
-

Today's stress signals

Breathing

SLOW ○ ○ ○ FAST

Mind

CALM ○ ○ ○ RACING

Concentration

FOCUSED ○ ○ ○ DISTRACTED

Switching off

SIMPLE ○ ○ ○ CHALLENGING

Today's stress danger rating

COOL ← → HOT

Reflect

Stressful moment

Did I 'turn the story around'? How?

Bird's-eye view

Tools I used

- ☐ BREATHE
- ☐ LEAVE
- ☐ MOVE
- ☐ OTHER

Today, I am feeling good about ...

Pause

Did I do my gratitude notes?

YES NO

Feeling before

Feeling after

Did I take a mindfulness pause?

YES NO

Feeling before

Feeling after

Pausing improved my stress

FROM /10 TO /10

Connect

3 moments of connection

1.

2.

3.

Person I'm grateful for (and why)

Today's thank you moment

Word of the day

DAY M T W T F S S

DATE / /

Check-in

Today's body feels

- ENERGETIC
- STRONG
- ACHY
- CAPABLE
- TIRED
- SLOW
-

Today's dominant vibe

- CALM
- OPTIMISTIC
- OKAY
- SAD
- NERVOUS
- SATISFIED
- ANGRY
- YEAH-NAH
-

Today's stress signals

Breathing

SLOW ○ ○ ○ FAST

Mind

CALM ○ ○ ○ RACING

Concentration

FOCUSED ○ ○ ○ DISTRACTED

Switching off

SIMPLE ○ ○ ○ CHALLENGING

Today's stress danger rating

COOL ← → HOT

Reflect

Stressful moment

Did I 'turn the story around'? How?

Bird's-eye view

Tools I used

- ☐ BREATHE
- ☐ LEAVE
- ☐ MOVE
- ☐ OTHER

Today, I am feeling good about ...

Pause

Did I do my gratitude notes?

YES NO

Feeling before

Feeling after

Did I take a mindfulness pause?

YES NO

Feeling before

Feeling after

Pausing improved my stress

FROM /10

TO /10

Connect

3 moments of connection

1.

2.

3.

Person I'm grateful for (and why)

Today's thank you moment

Word of the day

DAY M T W T F S S

DATE / /

Check-in

Today's body feels

- ENERGETIC
- STRONG
- ACHY
- CAPABLE
- TIRED
- SLOW
-

Today's dominant vibe

- CALM
- OPTIMISTIC
- OKAY
- SAD
- NERVOUS
- SATISFIED
- ANGRY
- YEAH-NAH
-

Today's stress signals

Breathing

SLOW ○ ○ ○ FAST

Mind

CALM ○ ○ ○ RACING

Concentration

FOCUSED ○ ○ ○ DISTRACTED

Switching off

SIMPLE ○ ○ ○ CHALLENGING

Today's stress danger rating

COOL ← → HOT

Reflect

Stressful moment

Did I 'turn the story around'? How?

Bird's-eye view

Tools I used

- ☐ BREATHE
- ☐ LEAVE
- ☐ MOVE
- ☐ OTHER

Today, I am feeling good about ...

Pause

Did I do my gratitude notes?

◯ YES ◯ NO

Feeling before

Feeling after

Did I take a mindfulness pause?

◯ YES ◯ NO

Feeling before

Feeling after

Pausing improved my stress

FROM /10 TO /10

Connect

3 moments of connection

1.

2.

3.

Person I'm grateful for (and why)

Today's thank you moment

Word of the day

DAY M T W T F S S

DATE / /

Check-in

Today's body feels

- ENERGETIC
- STRONG
- ACHY
- CAPABLE
- TIRED
- SLOW
-

Today's dominant vibe

- CALM
- OPTIMISTIC
- OKAY
- SAD
- NERVOUS
- SATISFIED
- ANGRY
- YEAH-NAH
-

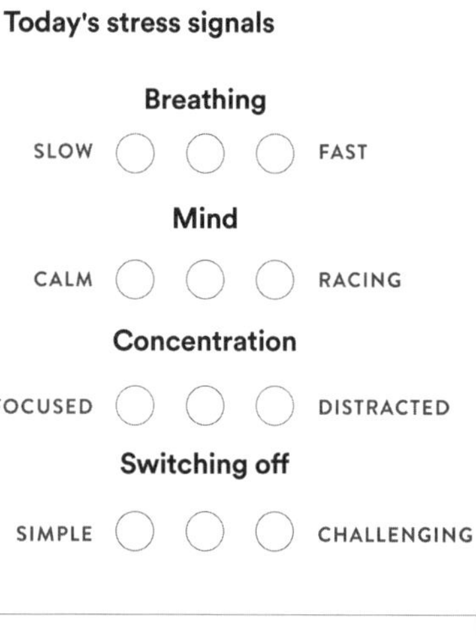

Today's stress danger rating

COOL ← → HOT

Reflect

Stressful moment

Did I 'turn the story around'? How?

Bird's-eye view

Tools I used

- [ ] BREATHE
- [ ] LEAVE
- [ ] MOVE
- [ ] OTHER

Today, I am feeling good about ...

Pause

Did I do my gratitude notes?

YES NO

Feeling before

Feeling after

Did I take a mindfulness pause?

YES NO

Feeling before

Feeling after

Pausing improved my stress

FROM /10

TO /10

Connect

3 moments of connection

1.

2.

3.

Person I'm grateful for (and why)

Today's thank you moment

Word of the day

DAY M T W T F S S

DATE / /

Check-in

Today's body feels

- ENERGETIC
- STRONG
- ACHY
- CAPABLE
- TIRED
- SLOW
-

Today's dominant vibe

- CALM
- OPTIMISTIC
- OKAY
- SAD
- NERVOUS
- SATISFIED
- ANGRY
- YEAH-NAH
-

Today's stress signals

Breathing

SLOW ○ ○ ○ FAST

Mind

CALM ○ ○ ○ RACING

Concentration

FOCUSED ○ ○ ○ DISTRACTED

Switching off

SIMPLE ○ ○ ○ CHALLENGING

Today's stress danger rating

COOL ← → HOT

Reflect

Stressful moment

Did I 'turn the story around'? How?

Bird's-eye view

Tools I used

☐ BREATHE

☐ LEAVE

☐ MOVE

☐ OTHER

Today, I am feeling good about ...

Pause

Did I do my gratitude notes?

YES NO

Feeling before

Feeling after

Did I take a mindfulness pause?

YES NO

Feeling before

Feeling after

Pausing improved my stress

FROM /10

TO /10

Connect

3 moments of connection

1.

2.

3.

Person I'm grateful for (and why)

Today's thank you moment

Word of the day

DAY M T W T F S S

DATE / /

Check-in

Today's body feels

- ENERGETIC
- STRONG
- ACHY
- CAPABLE
- TIRED
- SLOW
-

Today's dominant vibe

- CALM
- OPTIMISTIC
- OKAY
- SAD
- NERVOUS
- SATISFIED
- ANGRY
- YEAH-NAH
-

Today's stress signals

Breathing

SLOW ○ ○ ○ FAST

Mind

CALM ○ ○ ○ RACING

Concentration

FOCUSED ○ ○ ○ DISTRACTED

Switching off

SIMPLE ○ ○ ○ CHALLENGING

Today's stress danger rating

COOL ← → HOT

Reflect

Stressful moment

Did I 'turn the story around'? How?

Bird's-eye view

Tools I used

- ☐ BREATHE
- ☐ LEAVE
- ☐ MOVE
- ☐ OTHER

Today, I am feeling good about ...

Pause

Did I do my gratitude notes?

YES NO

Feeling before

Feeling after

Did I take a mindfulness pause?

YES NO

Feeling before

Feeling after

Pausing improved my stress

FROM /10 TO /10

Connect

3 moments of connection

1.

2.

3.

Person I'm grateful for (and why)

Today's thank you moment

Word of the day

DAY M T W T F S S

DATE / /

Check-in

Today's body feels

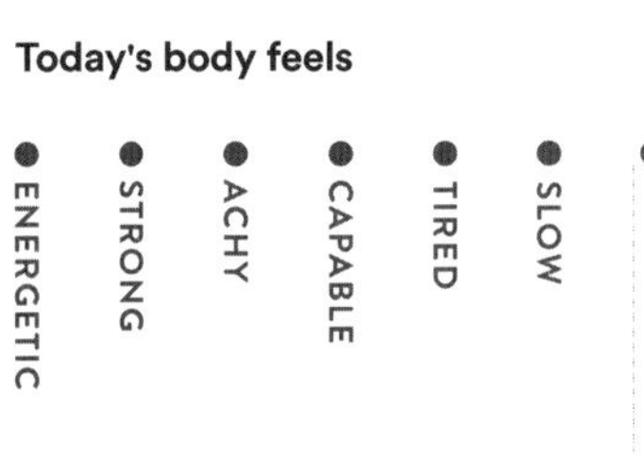

Today's dominant vibe

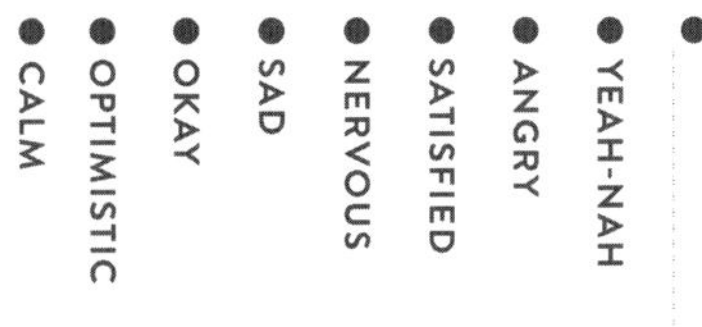

Today's stress signals

Breathing

SLOW ◯ ◯ ◯ FAST

Mind

CALM ◯ ◯ ◯ RACING

Concentration

FOCUSED ◯ ◯ ◯ DISTRACTED

Switching off

SIMPLE ◯ ◯ ◯ CHALLENGING

Today's stress danger rating

COOL ← → HOT

Reflect

Stressful moment

Did I 'turn the story around'? How?

Bird's-eye view

Tools I used

- ☐ BREATHE
- ☐ LEAVE
- ☐ MOVE
- ☐ OTHER

Today, I am feeling good about ...

Pause

Did I do my gratitude notes?

◯ YES ◯ NO

Feeling before

Feeling after

Did I take a mindfulness pause?

◯ YES ◯ NO

Feeling before

Feeling after

Pausing improved my stress

FROM /10 TO /10

Connect

3 moments of connection

1.

2.

3.

Person I'm grateful for (and why)

Today's thank you moment

Word of the day

DAY M T W T F S S

DATE / /

Check-in

Today's body feels

- ENERGETIC
- STRONG
- ACHY
- CAPABLE
- TIRED
- SLOW
-

Today's dominant vibe

- CALM
- OPTIMISTIC
- OKAY
- SAD
- NERVOUS
- SATISFIED
- ANGRY
- YEAH-NAH
-

Today's stress signals

Breathing

SLOW ○ ○ ○ FAST

Mind

CALM ○ ○ ○ RACING

Concentration

FOCUSED ○ ○ ○ DISTRACTED

Switching off

SIMPLE ○ ○ ○ CHALLENGING

Today's stress danger rating

COOL ← → HOT

Reflect

Stressful moment

Did I 'turn the story around'? How?

Bird's-eye view

Tools I used

- [ ] BREATHE
- [ ] LEAVE
- [ ] MOVE
- [ ] OTHER

Today, I am feeling good about ...

Pause

Did I do my gratitude notes?

◯ YES ◯ NO

Feeling before

Feeling after

Did I take a mindfulness pause?

◯ YES ◯ NO

Feeling before

Feeling after

Pausing improved my stress

FROM /10

TO /10

Connect

3 moments of connection

1.

2.

3.

Person I'm grateful for (and why)

Today's thank you moment

Word of the day

DAY M T W T F S S

DATE / /

Check-in

Today's body feels

- ENERGETIC
- STRONG
- ACHY
- CAPABLE
- TIRED
- SLOW
-

Today's dominant vibe

- CALM
- OPTIMISTIC
- OKAY
- SAD
- NERVOUS
- SATISFIED
- ANGRY
- YEAH-NAH
-

Today's stress signals

Breathing

SLOW ◯ ◯ ◯ FAST

Mind

CALM ◯ ◯ ◯ RACING

Concentration

FOCUSED ◯ ◯ ◯ DISTRACTED

Switching off

SIMPLE ◯ ◯ ◯ CHALLENGING

Today's stress danger rating

COOL ← → HOT

Reflect

Stressful moment

Did I 'turn the story around'? How?

Bird's-eye view

Tools I used

- [ ] BREATHE
- [ ] LEAVE
- [ ] MOVE
- [ ] OTHER

Today, I am feeling good about ...

Pause

Did I do my gratitude notes?

◯ YES ◯ NO

Feeling before

Feeling after

Did I take a mindfulness pause?

◯ YES ◯ NO

Feeling before

Feeling after

Pausing improved my stress

FROM /10

TO /10

Connect

3 moments of connection

1.

2.

3.

Person I'm grateful for (and why)

Today's thank you moment

Word of the day

DAY M T W T F S S

DATE / /

Check-in

Today's body feels

- ENERGETIC
- STRONG
- ACHY
- CAPABLE
- TIRED
- SLOW

Today's dominant vibe

- CALM
- OPTIMISTIC
- OKAY
- SAD
- NERVOUS
- SATISFIED
- ANGRY
- YEAH-NAH

Today's stress signals

Breathing

SLOW ○ ○ ○ FAST

Mind

CALM ○ ○ ○ RACING

Concentration

FOCUSED ○ ○ ○ DISTRACTED

Switching off

SIMPLE ○ ○ ○ CHALLENGING

Today's stress danger rating

COOL ← → HOT

Reflect

Stressful moment

Did I 'turn the story around'? How?

Bird's-eye view

Tools I used

- ☐ BREATHE
- ☐ LEAVE
- ☐ MOVE
- ☐ OTHER

Today, I am feeling good about ...

Pause

Did I do my gratitude notes?

YES NO

Feeling before

Feeling after

Did I take a mindfulness pause?

YES NO

Feeling before

Feeling after

Pausing improved my stress

FROM /10

TO /10

Connect

3 moments of connection

1.

2.

3.

Person I'm grateful for (and why)

Today's thank you moment

Word of the day

DAY M T W T F S S

DATE / /

Check-in

Today's body feels

- ENERGETIC
- STRONG
- ACHY
- CAPABLE
- TIRED
- SLOW
-

Today's dominant vibe

- CALM
- OPTIMISTIC
- OKAY
- SAD
- NERVOUS
- SATISFIED
- ANGRY
- YEAH-NAH
-

Today's stress signals

Breathing

SLOW ○ ○ ○ FAST

Mind

CALM ○ ○ ○ RACING

Concentration

FOCUSED ○ ○ ○ DISTRACTED

Switching off

SIMPLE ○ ○ ○ CHALLENGING

Today's stress danger rating

COOL ← → HOT

Reflect

Stressful moment

Did I 'turn the story around'? How?

Bird's-eye view

Tools I used

- [ ] BREATHE
- [ ] LEAVE
- [ ] MOVE
- [ ] OTHER

Today, I am feeling good about ...

Pause

Did I do my gratitude notes?

YES NO

Feeling before

Feeling after

Did I take a mindfulness pause?

YES NO

Feeling before

Feeling after

Pausing improved my stress

FROM /10

TO /10

Connect

3 moments of connection

1.

2.

3.

Person I'm grateful for (and why)

Today's thank you moment

Word of the day

DAY M T W T F S S

DATE / /

Check-in

Today's body feels

- ENERGETIC
- STRONG
- ACHY
- CAPABLE
- TIRED
- SLOW

Today's dominant vibe

- CALM
- OPTIMISTIC
- OKAY
- SAD
- NERVOUS
- SATISFIED
- ANGRY
- YEAH-NAH

Today's stress signals

Breathing

SLOW ○ ○ ○ FAST

Mind

CALM ○ ○ ○ RACING

Concentration

FOCUSED ○ ○ ○ DISTRACTED

Switching off

SIMPLE ○ ○ ○ CHALLENGING

Today's stress danger rating

COOL ← → HOT

Reflect

Stressful moment

Did I 'turn the story around'? How?

Bird's-eye view

Tools I used

- ☐ BREATHE
- ☐ LEAVE
- ☐ MOVE
- ☐ OTHER

Today, I am feeling good about ...

Pause

Did I do my gratitude notes?

◯ YES ◯ NO

Feeling before

Feeling after

Did I take a mindfulness pause?

◯ YES ◯ NO

Feeling before

Feeling after

Pausing improved my stress

FROM /10 TO /10

Connect

3 moments of connection

1.

2.

3.

Person I'm grateful for (and why)

Today's thank you moment

Word of the day

DAY M T W T F S S

DATE / /

Check-in

Today's body feels

- ENERGETIC
- STRONG
- ACHY
- CAPABLE
- TIRED
- SLOW
-

Today's dominant vibe

- CALM
- OPTIMISTIC
- OKAY
- SAD
- NERVOUS
- SATISFIED
- ANGRY
- YEAH-NAH
-

Today's stress signals

Breathing

SLOW ○ ○ ○ FAST

Mind

CALM ○ ○ ○ RACING

Concentration

FOCUSED ○ ○ ○ DISTRACTED

Switching off

SIMPLE ○ ○ ○ CHALLENGING

Today's stress danger rating

COOL ← → HOT

Reflect

Stressful moment

Did I 'turn the story around'? How?

Bird's-eye view

Tools I used

- ☐ BREATHE
- ☐ LEAVE
- ☐ MOVE
- ☐ OTHER

Today, I am feeling good about ...

Pause

Did I do my gratitude notes?

◯ YES ◯ NO

Feeling before

Feeling after

Did I take a mindfulness pause?

◯ YES ◯ NO

Feeling before

Feeling after

Pausing improved my stress

FROM /10

TO /10

Connect

3 moments of connection

1.

2.

3.

Person I'm grateful for (and why)

Today's thank you moment

Word of the day

DAY M T W T F S S

DATE / /

Check-in

Today's body feels

- ENERGETIC
- STRONG
- ACHY
- CAPABLE
- TIRED
- SLOW
-

Today's dominant vibe

- CALM
- OPTIMISTIC
- OKAY
- SAD
- NERVOUS
- SATISFIED
- ANGRY
- YEAH-NAH
-

Today's stress signals

Breathing

SLOW ○ ○ ○ FAST

Mind

CALM ○ ○ ○ RACING

Concentration

FOCUSED ○ ○ ○ DISTRACTED

Switching off

SIMPLE ○ ○ ○ CHALLENGING

Today's stress danger rating

COOL ← → HOT

Reflect

Stressful moment

Did I 'turn the story around'? How?

Bird's-eye view

Tools I used

- [ ] BREATHE
- [ ] LEAVE
- [ ] MOVE
- [ ] OTHER

Today, I am feeling good about ...

Pause

Did I do my gratitude notes?

◯ YES ◯ NO

Feeling before

Feeling after

Did I take a mindfulness pause?

◯ YES ◯ NO

Feeling before

Feeling after

Pausing improved my stress

FROM /10

TO /10

Connect

3 moments of connection

1.

2.

3.

Person I'm grateful for (and why)

Today's thank you moment

Word of the day

DAY M T W T F S S

DATE / /

Check-in

Today's body feels

- ENERGETIC
- STRONG
- ACHY
- CAPABLE
- TIRED
- SLOW
-

Today's dominant vibe

Today's stress signals

Breathing

SLOW ○ ○ ○ FAST

Mind

CALM ○ ○ ○ RACING

Concentration

FOCUSED ○ ○ ○ DISTRACTED

Switching off

SIMPLE ○ ○ ○ CHALLENGING

Today's stress danger rating

COOL ← → HOT

Reflect

Stressful moment

Did I 'turn the story around'? How?

Bird's-eye view

Tools I used

- ☐ BREATHE
- ☐ LEAVE
- ☐ MOVE
- ☐ OTHER

Today, I am feeling good about ...

Pause

Did I do my gratitude notes?

YES NO

Feeling before

Feeling after

Did I take a mindfulness pause?

YES NO

Feeling before

Feeling after

Pausing improved my stress

FROM /10 TO /10

Connect

3 moments of connection

1.

2.

3.

Person I'm grateful for (and why)

Today's thank you moment

Word of the day

DAY M T W T F S S

DATE / /

Check-in

Today's body feels

- ENERGETIC
- STRONG
- ACHY
- CAPABLE
- TIRED
- SLOW

Today's dominant vibe

- CALM
- OPTIMISTIC
- OKAY
- SAD
- NERVOUS
- SATISFIED
- ANGRY
- YEAH-NAH

Today's stress signals

Breathing

SLOW ○ ○ ○ FAST

Mind

CALM ○ ○ ○ RACING

Concentration

FOCUSED ○ ○ ○ DISTRACTED

Switching off

SIMPLE ○ ○ ○ CHALLENGING

Today's stress danger rating

COOL ← → HOT

Reflect

Stressful moment

Did I 'turn the story around'? How?

Bird's-eye view

Tools I used

- ☐ BREATHE
- ☐ LEAVE
- ☐ MOVE
- ☐ OTHER

Today, I am feeling good about ...

Pause

Did I do my gratitude notes?

YES NO

Feeling before

Feeling after

Did I take a mindfulness pause?

YES NO

Feeling before

Feeling after

Pausing improved my stress

FROM /10

TO /10

Connect

3 moments of connection

1.

2.

3.

Person I'm grateful for (and why)

Today's thank you moment

Word of the day

DAY M T W T F S S

DATE / /

Check-in

Today's body feels

- ENERGETIC
- STRONG
- ACHY
- CAPABLE
- TIRED
- SLOW

Today's dominant vibe

- CALM
- OPTIMISTIC
- OKAY
- SAD
- NERVOUS
- SATISFIED
- ANGRY
- YEAH-NAH

Today's stress signals

Breathing

SLOW ○ ○ ○ FAST

Mind

CALM ○ ○ ○ RACING

Concentration

FOCUSED ○ ○ ○ DISTRACTED

Switching off

SIMPLE ○ ○ ○ CHALLENGING

Today's stress danger rating

COOL ← → HOT

Reflect

Stressful moment

Did I 'turn the story around'? How?

Bird's-eye view

Tools I used

- [ ] BREATHE
- [ ] LEAVE
- [ ] MOVE
- [ ] OTHER

Today, I am feeling good about ...

Pause

Did I do my gratitude notes?

YES NO

Feeling before

Feeling after

Did I take a mindfulness pause?

YES NO

Feeling before

Feeling after

Pausing improved my stress

FROM /10

TO /10

Connect

3 moments of connection

1.

2.

3.

Person I'm grateful for (and why)

Today's thank you moment

Word of the day

DAY M T W T F S S

DATE / /

Check-in

Today's body feels

- ENERGETIC
- STRONG
- ACHY
- CAPABLE
- TIRED
- SLOW

Today's dominant vibe

- CALM
- OPTIMISTIC
- OKAY
- SAD
- NERVOUS
- SATISFIED
- ANGRY
- YEAH-NAH

Today's stress signals

Breathing

SLOW ◯ ◯ ◯ FAST

Mind

CALM ◯ ◯ ◯ RACING

Concentration

FOCUSED ◯ ◯ ◯ DISTRACTED

Switching off

SIMPLE ◯ ◯ ◯ CHALLENGING

Today's stress danger rating

COOL ← → HOT

Reflect

Stressful moment

Did I 'turn the story around'? How?

Bird's-eye view

Tools I used

- ☐ BREATHE
- ☐ LEAVE
- ☐ MOVE
- ☐ OTHER

Today, I am feeling good about ...

Pause

Did I do my gratitude notes?

◯ YES ◯ NO

Feeling before

Feeling after

Did I take a mindfulness pause?

◯ YES ◯ NO

Feeling before

Feeling after

Pausing improved my stress

FROM /10 TO /10

Connect

3 moments of connection

1.

2.

3.

Person I'm grateful for (and why)

Today's thank you moment

Word of the day

DAY M T W T F S S

DATE / /

Check-in

Today's body feels

- ENERGETIC
- STRONG
- ACHY
- CAPABLE
- TIRED
- SLOW
-

Today's dominant vibe

- CALM
- OPTIMISTIC
- OKAY
- SAD
- NERVOUS
- SATISFIED
- ANGRY
- YEAH-NAH
-

Today's stress signals

Breathing

SLOW ◯ ◯ ◯ FAST

Mind

CALM ◯ ◯ ◯ RACING

Concentration

FOCUSED ◯ ◯ ◯ DISTRACTED

Switching off

SIMPLE ◯ ◯ ◯ CHALLENGING

Today's stress danger rating

COOL ← → HOT

Reflect

Stressful moment

Did I 'turn the story around'? How?

Bird's-eye view

Tools I used

☐ BREATHE

☐ LEAVE

☐ MOVE

☐ OTHER

Today, I am feeling good about ...

Pause

Did I do my gratitude notes?

YES NO

Feeling before

Feeling after

Did I take a mindfulness pause?

YES NO

Feeling before

Feeling after

Pausing improved my stress

FROM /10 TO /10

Connect

3 moments of connection

1.

2.

3.

Person I'm grateful for (and why)

Today's thank you moment

Word of the day

DAY M T W T F S S

DATE / /

Check-in

Today's body feels

- ENERGETIC
- STRONG
- ACHY
- CAPABLE
- TIRED
- SLOW
-

Today's dominant vibe

- CALM
- OPTIMISTIC
- OKAY
- SAD
- NERVOUS
- SATISFIED
- ANGRY
- YEAH-NAH
-

Today's stress signals

Breathing

SLOW ○ ○ ○ FAST

Mind

CALM ○ ○ ○ RACING

Concentration

FOCUSED ○ ○ ○ DISTRACTED

Switching off

SIMPLE ○ ○ ○ CHALLENGING

Today's stress danger rating

COOL ← → HOT

Reflect

Stressful moment

Did I 'turn the story around'? How?

Bird's-eye view

Tools I used

- ☐ BREATHE
- ☐ LEAVE
- ☐ MOVE
- ☐ OTHER

Today, I am feeling good about ...

Pause

Did I do my gratitude notes?

◯ YES ◯ NO

Feeling before

Feeling after

Did I take a mindfulness pause?

◯ YES ◯ NO

Feeling before

Feeling after

Pausing improved my stress

FROM /10

TO /10

Connect

3 moments of connection

1.

2.

3.

Person I'm grateful for (and why)

Today's thank you moment

Word of the day

DAY M T W T F S S

DATE / /

Check-in

Today's body feels

- ENERGETIC
- STRONG
- ACHY
- CAPABLE
- TIRED
- SLOW
-

Today's dominant vibe

- CALM
- OPTIMISTIC
- OKAY
- SAD
- NERVOUS
- SATISFIED
- ANGRY
- YEAH-NAH
-

Today's stress signals

Breathing

SLOW ○ ○ ○ FAST

Mind

CALM ○ ○ ○ RACING

Concentration

FOCUSED ○ ○ ○ DISTRACTED

Switching off

SIMPLE ○ ○ ○ CHALLENGING

Today's stress danger rating

COOL ← → HOT

Reflect

Stressful moment

Did I 'turn the story around'? How?

Bird's-eye view

Tools I used

- ☐ BREATHE
- ☐ LEAVE
- ☐ MOVE
- ☐ OTHER

Today, I am feeling good about ...

Pause

Did I do my gratitude notes?

◯ YES ◯ NO

Feeling before

Feeling after

Did I take a mindfulness pause?

◯ YES ◯ NO

Feeling before

Feeling after

Pausing improved my stress

FROM /10 TO /10

Connect

3 moments of connection

1.

2.

3.

Person I'm grateful for (and why)

Today's thank you moment

Word of the day

DAY M T W T F S S

DATE / /

Check-in

Today's body feels

- ENERGETIC
- STRONG
- ACHY
- CAPABLE
- TIRED
- SLOW
-

Today's dominant vibe

- CALM
- OPTIMISTIC
- OKAY
- SAD
- NERVOUS
- SATISFIED
- ANGRY
- YEAH-NAH
-

Today's stress signals

Breathing

SLOW ○ ○ ○ FAST

Mind

CALM ○ ○ ○ RACING

Concentration

FOCUSED ○ ○ ○ DISTRACTED

Switching off

SIMPLE ○ ○ ○ CHALLENGING

Today's stress danger rating

COOL ← → HOT

Reflect

Stressful moment

Did I 'turn the story around'? How?

Bird's-eye view

Tools I used

- ☐ BREATHE
- ☐ LEAVE
- ☐ MOVE
- ☐ OTHER

Today, I am feeling good about ...

Pause

Did I do my gratitude notes?

◯ YES ◯ NO

Feeling before

Feeling after

Did I take a mindfulness pause?

◯ YES ◯ NO

Feeling before

Feeling after

Pausing improved my stress

FROM /10 TO /10

Connect

3 moments of connection

1.

2.

3.

Person I'm grateful for (and why)

Today's thank you moment

Word of the day

DAY M T W T F S S

DATE / /

Check-in

Today's body feels

- ENERGETIC
- STRONG
- ACHY
- CAPABLE
- TIRED
- SLOW

Today's dominant vibe

- CALM
- OPTIMISTIC
- OKAY
- SAD
- NERVOUS
- SATISFIED
- ANGRY
- YEAH-NAH

Today's stress signals

Breathing

SLOW ○ ○ ○ FAST

Mind

CALM ○ ○ ○ RACING

Concentration

FOCUSED ○ ○ ○ DISTRACTED

Switching off

SIMPLE ○ ○ ○ CHALLENGING

Today's stress danger rating

COOL ← → HOT

Reflect

Stressful moment

Did I 'turn the story around'? How?

Bird's-eye view

Tools I used

- ☐ BREATHE
- ☐ LEAVE
- ☐ MOVE
- ☐ OTHER

Today, I am feeling good about ...

Pause

Did I do my gratitude notes?

◯ YES ◯ NO

Feeling before

Feeling after

Did I take a mindfulness pause?

◯ YES ◯ NO

Feeling before

Feeling after

Pausing improved my stress

FROM /10

TO /10

Connect

3 moments of connection

1.

2.

3.

Person I'm grateful for (and why)

Today's thank you moment

Word of the day

DAY M T W T F S S

DATE / /

Check-in

Today's body feels

- ENERGETIC
- STRONG
- ACHY
- CAPABLE
- TIRED
- SLOW

Today's dominant vibe

- CALM
- OPTIMISTIC
- OKAY
- SAD
- NERVOUS
- SATISFIED
- ANGRY
- YEAH-NAH

Today's stress signals

Breathing

SLOW ○ ○ ○ FAST

Mind

CALM ○ ○ ○ RACING

Concentration

FOCUSED ○ ○ ○ DISTRACTED

Switching off

SIMPLE ○ ○ ○ CHALLENGING

Today's stress danger rating

COOL ← → HOT

Reflect

Stressful moment

Did I 'turn the story around'? How?

Bird's-eye view

Tools I used

- [ ] BREATHE
- [ ] LEAVE
- [ ] MOVE
- [ ] OTHER

Today, I am feeling good about ...

Pause

Did I do my gratitude notes?

◯ YES ◯ NO

Feeling before

Feeling after

Did I take a mindfulness pause?

◯ YES ◯ NO

Feeling before

Feeling after

Pausing improved my stress

FROM /10 TO /10

Connect

3 moments of connection

1.

2.

3.

Person I'm grateful for (and why)

Today's thank you moment

Word of the day

DAY M T W T F S S

DATE / /

Check-in

Today's body feels

ENERGETIC
STRONG
ACHY
CAPABLE
TIRED
SLOW

Today's dominant vibe

CALM
OPTIMISTIC
OKAY
SAD
NERVOUS
SATISFIED
ANGRY
YEAH-NAH

Today's stress signals

Breathing

SLOW ◯ ◯ ◯ FAST

Mind

CALM ◯ ◯ ◯ RACING

Concentration

FOCUSED ◯ ◯ ◯ DISTRACTED

Switching off

SIMPLE ◯ ◯ ◯ CHALLENGING

Today's stress danger rating

COOL ← → HOT

Reflect

Stressful moment

Did I 'turn the story around'? How?

Bird's-eye view

Tools I used

- [ ] BREATHE
- [ ] LEAVE
- [ ] MOVE
- [ ] OTHER

Today, I am feeling good about ...

Pause

Did I do my gratitude notes?

◯ YES ◯ NO

Feeling before

Feeling after

Did I take a mindfulness pause?

◯ YES ◯ NO

Feeling before

Feeling after

Pausing improved my stress

FROM /10

TO /10

Connect

3 moments of connection

1.

2.

3.

Person I'm grateful for (and why)

Today's thank you moment

Word of the day

DAY M T W T F S S

DATE / /

Check-in

Today's body feels

- ENERGETIC
- STRONG
- ACHY
- CAPABLE
- TIRED
- SLOW
-

Today's dominant vibe

- CALM
- OPTIMISTIC
- OKAY
- SAD
- NERVOUS
- SATISFIED
- ANGRY
- YEAH-NAH
-

Today's stress signals

Breathing

SLOW ○ ○ ○ FAST

Mind

CALM ○ ○ ○ RACING

Concentration

FOCUSED ○ ○ ○ DISTRACTED

Switching off

SIMPLE ○ ○ ○ CHALLENGING

Today's stress danger rating

COOL ← → HOT

Reflect

Stressful moment

Did I 'turn the story around'? How?

Bird's-eye view

Tools I used

- [ ] BREATHE
- [ ] LEAVE
- [ ] MOVE
- [ ] OTHER

Today, I am feeling good about ...

Pause

Did I do my gratitude notes?

◯ YES ◯ NO

Feeling before

Feeling after

Did I take a mindfulness pause?

◯ YES ◯ NO

Feeling before

Feeling after

Pausing improved my stress

FROM /10

TO /10

Connect

3 moments of connection

1.

2.

3.

Person I'm grateful for (and why)

Today's thank you moment

Word of the day

DAY M T W T F S S

DATE / /

Check-in

Today's body feels

- ENERGETIC
- STRONG
- ACHY
- CAPABLE
- TIRED
- SLOW
-

Today's dominant vibe

- CALM
- OPTIMISTIC
- OKAY
- SAD
- NERVOUS
- SATISFIED
- ANGRY
- YEAH-NAH
-

Today's stress signals

Breathing

SLOW ○ ○ ○ FAST

Mind

CALM ○ ○ ○ RACING

Concentration

FOCUSED ○ ○ ○ DISTRACTED

Switching off

SIMPLE ○ ○ ○ CHALLENGING

Today's stress danger rating

COOL ← → HOT

Reflect

Stressful moment

Did I 'turn the story around'? How?

Bird's-eye view

Tools I used

- ☐ BREATHE
- ☐ LEAVE
- ☐ MOVE
- ☐ OTHER

Today, I am feeling good about ...

Pause

Did I do my gratitude notes?

◯ YES ◯ NO

Feeling before

Feeling after

Did I take a mindfulness pause?

◯ YES ◯ NO

Feeling before

Feeling after

Pausing improved my stress

FROM /10

TO /10

Connect

3 moments of connection

1.

2.

3.

Person I'm grateful for (and why)

Today's thank you moment

Word of the day

DAY M T W T F S S

DATE / /

Check-in

Today's body feels

- ENERGETIC
- STRONG
- ACHY
- CAPABLE
- TIRED
- SLOW
-

Today's dominant vibe

- CALM
- OPTIMISTIC
- OKAY
- SAD
- NERVOUS
- SATISFIED
- ANGRY
- YEAH-NAH
-

Today's stress signals

Breathing

SLOW ○ ○ ○ FAST

Mind

CALM ○ ○ ○ RACING

Concentration

FOCUSED ○ ○ ○ DISTRACTED

Switching off

SIMPLE ○ ○ ○ CHALLENGING

Today's stress danger rating

COOL ← → HOT

Reflect

Stressful moment

Did I 'turn the story around'? How?

Bird's-eye view

Tools I used

- ☐ BREATHE
- ☐ LEAVE
- ☐ MOVE
- ☐ OTHER

Today, I am feeling good about ...

Pause

Did I do my gratitude notes?

YES NO

Feeling before

Feeling after

Did I take a mindfulness pause?

YES NO

Feeling before

Feeling after

Pausing improved my stress

FROM /10 TO /10

Connect

3 moments of connection

1.

2.

3.

Person I'm grateful for (and why)

Today's thank you moment

Word of the day

DAY M T W T F S S

DATE / /

Check-in

Today's body feels

- ENERGETIC
- STRONG
- ACHY
- CAPABLE
- TIRED
- SLOW
-

Today's dominant vibe

- CALM
- OPTIMISTIC
- OKAY
- SAD
- NERVOUS
- SATISFIED
- ANGRY
- YEAH-NAH
-

Today's stress signals

Breathing

SLOW ○ ○ ○ FAST

Mind

CALM ○ ○ ○ RACING

Concentration

FOCUSED ○ ○ ○ DISTRACTED

Switching off

SIMPLE ○ ○ ○ CHALLENGING

Today's stress danger rating

COOL ← → HOT

Reflect

Stressful moment

Did I 'turn the story around'? How?

Bird's-eye view

Tools I used

- [ ] BREATHE
- [ ] LEAVE
- [ ] MOVE
- [ ] OTHER

Today, I am feeling good about ...

Pause

Did I do my gratitude notes?

YES NO

Feeling before

Feeling after

Did I take a mindfulness pause?

YES NO

Feeling before

Feeling after

Pausing improved my stress

FROM /10 TO /10

Connect

3 moments of connection

1.

2.

3.

Person I'm grateful for (and why)

Today's thank you moment

Word of the day

DAY M T W T F S S

DATE / /

Check-in

Today's body feels

- ENERGETIC
- STRONG
- ACHY
- CAPABLE
- TIRED
- SLOW
-

Today's dominant vibe

- CALM
- OPTIMISTIC
- OKAY
- SAD
- NERVOUS
- SATISFIED
- ANGRY
- YEAH-NAH
-

Today's stress signals

Breathing

SLOW ○ ○ ○ FAST

Mind

CALM ○ ○ ○ RACING

Concentration

FOCUSED ○ ○ ○ DISTRACTED

Switching off

SIMPLE ○ ○ ○ CHALLENGING

Today's stress danger rating

COOL ← → HOT

Reflect

Stressful moment

Did I 'turn the story around'? How?

Bird's-eye view

Tools I used

- ☐ BREATHE
- ☐ LEAVE
- ☐ MOVE
- ☐ OTHER

Today, I am feeling good about ...

Pause

Did I do my gratitude notes?

◯ YES ◯ NO

Feeling before

Feeling after

Did I take a mindfulness pause?

◯ YES ◯ NO

Feeling before

Feeling after

Pausing improved my stress

FROM /10

TO /10

Connect

3 moments of connection

1.

2.

3.

Person I'm grateful for (and why)

Today's thank you moment

Word of the day

DAY M T W T F S S

DATE / /

Check-in

Today's body feels

- ENERGETIC
- STRONG
- ACHY
- CAPABLE
- TIRED
- SLOW
-

Today's dominant vibe

- CALM
- OPTIMISTIC
- OKAY
- SAD
- NERVOUS
- SATISFIED
- ANGRY
- YEAH-NAH
-

Today's stress signals

Breathing

SLOW ○ ○ ○ FAST

Mind

CALM ○ ○ ○ RACING

Concentration

FOCUSED ○ ○ ○ DISTRACTED

Switching off

SIMPLE ○ ○ ○ CHALLENGING

Today's stress danger rating

COOL ← → HOT

Reflect

Stressful moment

Did I 'turn the story around'? How?

Bird's-eye view

Tools I used

- ☐ BREATHE
- ☐ LEAVE
- ☐ MOVE
- ☐ OTHER

Today, I am feeling good about ...

Pause

Did I do my gratitude notes?

◯ YES ◯ NO

Feeling before

Feeling after

Did I take a mindfulness pause?

◯ YES ◯ NO

Feeling before

Feeling after

Pausing improved my stress

FROM /10 TO /10

Connect

3 moments of connection

1.

2.

3.

Person I'm grateful for (and why)

Today's thank you moment

Word of the day

DAY M T W T F S S

DATE / /

Check-in

Today's body feels

- ENERGETIC
- STRONG
- ACHY
- CAPABLE
- TIRED
- SLOW
-

Today's dominant vibe

- CALM
- OPTIMISTIC
- OKAY
- SAD
- NERVOUS
- SATISFIED
- ANGRY
- YEAH-NAH
-

Today's stress signals

Breathing

SLOW ○ ○ ○ FAST

Mind

CALM ○ ○ ○ RACING

Concentration

FOCUSED ○ ○ ○ DISTRACTED

Switching off

SIMPLE ○ ○ ○ CHALLENGING

Today's stress danger rating

COOL ← → HOT

Reflect

Stressful moment

Did I 'turn the story around'? How?

Bird's-eye view

Tools I used

- [ ] BREATHE
- [ ] LEAVE
- [ ] MOVE
- [ ] OTHER

Today, I am feeling good about ...

Pause

Did I do my gratitude notes?

YES NO

Feeling before

Feeling after

Did I take a mindfulness pause?

YES NO

Feeling before

Feeling after

Pausing improved my stress

FROM /10 TO /10

Connect

3 moments of connection

1.

2.

3.

Person I'm grateful for (and why)

Today's thank you moment

Word of the day

DAY M T W T F S S

DATE / /

Check-in

Today's body feels

- ENERGETIC
- STRONG
- ACHY
- CAPABLE
- TIRED
- SLOW
-

Today's dominant vibe

- CALM
- OPTIMISTIC
- OKAY
- SAD
- NERVOUS
- SATISFIED
- ANGRY
- YEAH-NAH
-

Today's stress signals

Breathing

SLOW ○ ○ ○ FAST

Mind

CALM ○ ○ ○ RACING

Concentration

FOCUSED ○ ○ ○ DISTRACTED

Switching off

SIMPLE ○ ○ ○ CHALLENGING

Today's stress danger rating

COOL ← → HOT

Reflect

Stressful moment

Did I 'turn the story around'? How?

Bird's-eye view

Tools I used

- ☐ BREATHE
- ☐ LEAVE
- ☐ MOVE
- ☐ OTHER

Today, I am feeling good about ...

Pause

Did I do my gratitude notes?

◯ YES ◯ NO

Feeling before

Feeling after

Did I take a mindfulness pause?

◯ YES ◯ NO

Feeling before

Feeling after

Pausing improved my stress

FROM /10

TO /10

Connect

3 moments of connection

1.

2.

3.

Person I'm grateful for (and why)

Today's thank you moment

Word of the day

DAY M T W T F S S

DATE / /

Check-in

Today's body feels

- ENERGETIC
- STRONG
- ACHY
- CAPABLE
- TIRED
- SLOW

Today's dominant vibe

- CALM
- OPTIMISTIC
- OKAY
- SAD
- NERVOUS
- SATISFIED
- ANGRY
- YEAH-NAH

Today's stress signals

Breathing

SLOW ○ ○ ○ FAST

Mind

CALM ○ ○ ○ RACING

Concentration

FOCUSED ○ ○ ○ DISTRACTED

Switching off

SIMPLE ○ ○ ○ CHALLENGING

Today's stress danger rating

COOL ← → HOT

Reflect

Stressful moment

Did I 'turn the story around'? How?

Bird's-eye view

Tools I used

- ☐ BREATHE
- ☐ LEAVE
- ☐ MOVE
- ☐ OTHER

Today, I am feeling good about ...

Pause

Did I do my gratitude notes?

YES NO

Feeling before

Feeling after

Did I take a mindfulness pause?

YES NO

Feeling before

Feeling after

Pausing improved my stress

FROM /10 TO /10

Connect

3 moments of connection

1.

2.

3.

Person I'm grateful for (and why)

Today's thank you moment

Word of the day

DAY M T W T F S S

DATE / /

Check-in

Today's body feels

- ENERGETIC
- STRONG
- ACHY
- CAPABLE
- TIRED
- SLOW
-

Today's dominant vibe

- CALM
- OPTIMISTIC
- OKAY
- SAD
- NERVOUS
- SATISFIED
- ANGRY
- YEAH-NAH
-

Today's stress signals

Breathing

SLOW ○ ○ ○ FAST

Mind

CALM ○ ○ ○ RACING

Concentration

FOCUSED ○ ○ ○ DISTRACTED

Switching off

SIMPLE ○ ○ ○ CHALLENGING

Today's stress danger rating

COOL ← → HOT

Reflect

Stressful moment

Did I 'turn the story around'? How?

Bird's-eye view

Tools I used

- ☐ BREATHE
- ☐ LEAVE
- ☐ MOVE
- ☐ OTHER

Today, I am feeling good about ...

Pause

Did I do my gratitude notes?

YES NO

Feeling before

Feeling after

Did I take a mindfulness pause?

YES NO

Feeling before

Feeling after

Pausing improved my stress

FROM /10

TO /10

Connect

3 moments of connection

1.

2.

3.

Person I'm grateful for (and why)

Today's thank you moment

Word of the day

DAY M T W T F S S

DATE / /

Check-in

Today's body feels

- ENERGETIC
- STRONG
- ACHY
- CAPABLE
- TIRED
- SLOW

Today's dominant vibe

- CALM
- OPTIMISTIC
- OKAY
- SAD
- NERVOUS
- SATISFIED
- ANGRY
- YEAH-NAH

Today's stress signals

Breathing

SLOW ○ ○ ○ FAST

Mind

CALM ○ ○ ○ RACING

Concentration

FOCUSED ○ ○ ○ DISTRACTED

Switching off

SIMPLE ○ ○ ○ CHALLENGING

Today's stress danger rating

COOL ← → HOT

Reflect

Stressful moment

Did I 'turn the story around'? How?

Bird's-eye view

Tools I used

- ☐ BREATHE
- ☐ LEAVE
- ☐ MOVE
- ☐ OTHER

Today, I am feeling good about ...

Pause

Did I do my gratitude notes?

YES NO

Feeling before

Feeling after

Did I take a mindfulness pause?

YES NO

Feeling before

Feeling after

Pausing improved my stress

FROM /10

TO /10

Connect

3 moments of connection

1.

2.

3.

Person I'm grateful for (and why)

Today's thank you moment

Word of the day

DAY M T W T F S S

DATE / /

Check-in

Today's body feels

- ENERGETIC
- STRONG
- ACHY
- CAPABLE
- TIRED
- SLOW
-

Today's dominant vibe

- CALM
- OPTIMISTIC
- OKAY
- SAD
- NERVOUS
- SATISFIED
- ANGRY
- YEAH-NAH
-

Today's stress signals

Breathing

SLOW ○ ○ ○ FAST

Mind

CALM ○ ○ ○ RACING

Concentration

FOCUSED ○ ○ ○ DISTRACTED

Switching off

SIMPLE ○ ○ ○ CHALLENGING

Today's stress danger rating

COOL ← → HOT

Reflect

Stressful moment

Did I 'turn the story around'? How?

Bird's-eye view

Tools I used

- ☐ BREATHE
- ☐ LEAVE
- ☐ MOVE
- ☐ OTHER

Today, I am feeling good about ...

Pause

Did I do my gratitude notes?

YES NO

Feeling before

Feeling after

Did I take a mindfulness pause?

YES NO

Feeling before

Feeling after

Pausing improved my stress

FROM /10

TO /10

Connect

3 moments of connection

1.

2.

3.

Person I'm grateful for (and why)

Today's thank you moment

Word of the day

DAY M T W T F S S

DATE / /

Check-in

Today's body feels

ENERGETIC
STRONG
ACHY
CAPABLE
TIRED
SLOW

Today's dominant vibe

CALM
OPTIMISTIC
OKAY
SAD
NERVOUS
SATISFIED
ANGRY
YEAH-NAH

Today's stress signals

Breathing

SLOW ○ ○ ○ FAST

Mind

CALM ○ ○ ○ RACING

Concentration

FOCUSED ○ ○ ○ DISTRACTED

Switching off

SIMPLE ○ ○ ○ CHALLENGING

Today's stress danger rating

COOL ← → HOT

Reflect

Stressful moment

Did I 'turn the story around'? How?

Bird's-eye view

Tools I used

- [ ] BREATHE
- [ ] LEAVE
- [ ] MOVE
- [ ] OTHER

Today, I am feeling good about ...

Pause

Did I do my gratitude notes?

◯ YES ◯ NO

Feeling before

Feeling after

Did I take a mindfulness pause?

◯ YES ◯ NO

Feeling before

Feeling after

Pausing improved my stress

FROM /10 TO /10

Connect

3 moments of connection

1.

2.

3.

Person I'm grateful for (and why)

Today's thank you moment

Word of the day

DAY M T W T F S S

DATE / /

Check-in

Today's body feels

- ENERGETIC
- STRONG
- ACHY
- CAPABLE
- TIRED
- SLOW

Today's dominant vibe

- CALM
- OPTIMISTIC
- OKAY
- SAD
- NERVOUS
- SATISFIED
- ANGRY
- YEAH-NAH

Today's stress signals

Breathing

SLOW ○ ○ ○ FAST

Mind

CALM ○ ○ ○ RACING

Concentration

FOCUSED ○ ○ ○ DISTRACTED

Switching off

SIMPLE ○ ○ ○ CHALLENGING

Today's stress danger rating

COOL ← → HOT

Reflect

Stressful moment

Did I 'turn the story around'? How?

Bird's-eye view

Tools I used

- ☐ BREATHE
- ☐ LEAVE
- ☐ MOVE
- ☐ OTHER

Today, I am feeling good about ...

Pause

Did I do my gratitude notes?

◯ YES ◯ NO

Feeling before

Feeling after

Did I take a mindfulness pause?

◯ YES ◯ NO

Feeling before

Feeling after

Pausing improved my stress

FROM /10

TO /10

Connect

3 moments of connection

1.

2.

3.

Person I'm grateful for (and why)

Today's thank you moment

Word of the day

DAY M T W T F S S

DATE / /

Check-in

Today's body feels

- ENERGETIC
- STRONG
- ACHY
- CAPABLE
- TIRED
- SLOW
-

Today's dominant vibe

- CALM
- OPTIMISTIC
- OKAY
- SAD
- NERVOUS
- SATISFIED
- ANGRY
- YEAH-NAH
-

Today's stress signals

Breathing

SLOW ○ ○ ○ FAST

Mind

CALM ○ ○ ○ RACING

Concentration

FOCUSED ○ ○ ○ DISTRACTED

Switching off

SIMPLE ○ ○ ○ CHALLENGING

Today's stress danger rating

COOL ← → HOT

Reflect

Stressful moment

Did I 'turn the story around'? How?

Bird's-eye view

Tools I used

- ☐ BREATHE
- ☐ LEAVE
- ☐ MOVE
- ☐ OTHER

Today, I am feeling good about ...

Pause

Did I do my gratitude notes?

YES NO

Feeling before

Feeling after

Did I take a mindfulness pause?

YES NO

Feeling before

Feeling after

Pausing improved my stress

FROM /10

TO /10

Connect

3 moments of connection

1.

2.

3.

Person I'm grateful for (and why)

Today's thank you moment

Word of the day

DAY M T W T F S S

DATE / /

Check-in

Today's body feels

- ENERGETIC
- STRONG
- ACHY
- CAPABLE
- TIRED
- SLOW

Today's dominant vibe

- CALM
- OPTIMISTIC
- OKAY
- SAD
- NERVOUS
- SATISFIED
- ANGRY
- YEAH-NAH

Today's stress signals

Breathing

SLOW ◯ ◯ ◯ FAST

Mind

CALM ◯ ◯ ◯ RACING

Concentration

FOCUSED ◯ ◯ ◯ DISTRACTED

Switching off

SIMPLE ◯ ◯ ◯ CHALLENGING

Today's stress danger rating

COOL ← → HOT

Reflect

Stressful moment

Did I 'turn the story around'? How?

Bird's-eye view

Tools I used

- ☐ BREATHE
- ☐ LEAVE
- ☐ MOVE
- ☐ OTHER

Today, I am feeling good about ...

Pause

Did I do my gratitude notes?

◯ YES ◯ NO

Feeling before

Feeling after

Did I take a mindfulness pause?

◯ YES ◯ NO

Feeling before

Feeling after

Pausing improved my stress

FROM /10 TO /10

Connect

3 moments of connection

1.

2.

3.

Person I'm grateful for (and why)

Today's thank you moment

Word of the day

DAY M T W T F S S

DATE / /

Check-in

Today's body feels

- ENERGETIC
- STRONG
- ACHY
- CAPABLE
- TIRED
- SLOW
-

Today's dominant vibe

- CALM
- OPTIMISTIC
- OKAY
- SAD
- NERVOUS
- SATISFIED
- ANGRY
- YEAH-NAH
-

Today's stress signals

Breathing

SLOW ○ ○ ○ FAST

Mind

CALM ○ ○ ○ RACING

Concentration

FOCUSED ○ ○ ○ DISTRACTED

Switching off

SIMPLE ○ ○ ○ CHALLENGING

Today's stress danger rating

COOL ← → HOT

Reflect

Stressful moment

Did I 'turn the story around'? How?

Bird's-eye view

Tools I used

- [ ] BREATHE
- [ ] LEAVE
- [ ] MOVE
- [ ] OTHER

Today, I am feeling good about ...

Pause

Did I do my gratitude notes?

◯ YES ◯ NO

Feeling before

Feeling after

Did I take a mindfulness pause?

◯ YES ◯ NO

Feeling before

Feeling after

Pausing improved my stress

FROM /10 TO /10

Connect

3 moments of connection

1.

2.

3.

Person I'm grateful for (and why)

Today's thank you moment

Word of the day

DAY M T W T F S S

DATE / /

Check-in

Today's body feels

- ENERGETIC
- STRONG
- ACHY
- CAPABLE
- TIRED
- SLOW

Today's dominant vibe

- CALM
- OPTIMISTIC
- OKAY
- SAD
- NERVOUS
- SATISFIED
- ANGRY
- YEAH-NAH

Today's stress signals

Breathing

SLOW ○ ○ ○ FAST

Mind

CALM ○ ○ ○ RACING

Concentration

FOCUSED ○ ○ ○ DISTRACTED

Switching off

SIMPLE ○ ○ ○ CHALLENGING

Today's stress danger rating

COOL ← → HOT

Reflect

Stressful moment

Did I 'turn the story around'? How?

Bird's-eye view

Tools I used

- ☐ BREATHE
- ☐ LEAVE
- ☐ MOVE
- ☐ OTHER

Today, I am feeling good about ...

Pause

Did I do my gratitude notes?

YES NO

Feeling before

Feeling after

Did I take a mindfulness pause?

YES NO

Feeling before

Feeling after

Pausing improved my stress

FROM /10

TO /10

Connect

3 moments of connection

1.

2.

3.

Person I'm grateful for (and why)

Today's thank you moment

Word of the day

DAY M T W T F S S

DATE / /

Check-in

Today's body feels

Today's dominant vibe

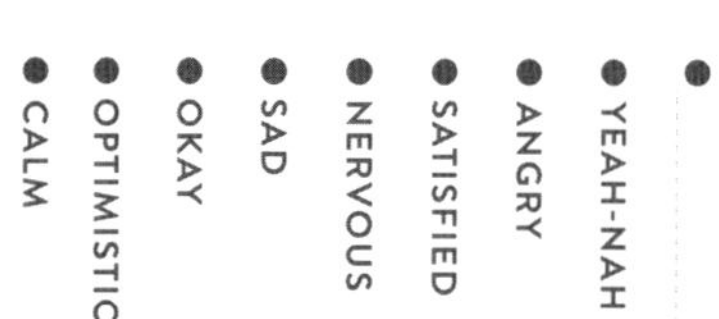

Today's stress signals

Today's stress danger rating

COOL ← → HOT

Reflect

Stressful moment

Did I 'turn the story around'? How?

Bird's-eye view

Tools I used

- [ ] BREATHE
- [ ] LEAVE
- [ ] MOVE
- [ ] OTHER

Today, I am feeling good about ...

Pause

Did I do my gratitude notes?

YES NO

Feeling before

Feeling after

Did I take a mindfulness pause?

YES NO

Feeling before

Feeling after

Pausing improved my stress

FROM /10

TO /10

Connect

3 moments of connection

1.

2.

3.

Person I'm grateful for (and why)

Today's thank you moment

Word of the day

DAY M T W T F S S

DATE / /

Check-in

Today's body feels

- ENERGETIC
- STRONG
- ACHY
- CAPABLE
- TIRED
- SLOW
-

Today's dominant vibe

- CALM
- OPTIMISTIC
- OKAY
- SAD
- NERVOUS
- SATISFIED
- ANGRY
- YEAH-NAH
-

Today's stress signals

Today's stress danger rating

COOL ← → HOT

Reflect

Stressful moment

Did I 'turn the story around'? How?

Bird's-eye view

Tools I used

- [ ] BREATHE
- [ ] LEAVE
- [ ] MOVE
- [ ] OTHER

Today, I am feeling good about ...

Pause

Did I do my gratitude notes?

YES NO

Feeling before

Feeling after

Did I take a mindfulness pause?

YES NO

Feeling before

Feeling after

Pausing improved my stress

FROM /10

TO /10

Connect

3 moments of connection

1.

2.

3.

Person I'm grateful for (and why)

Today's thank you moment

Word of the day

DAY M T W T F S S

DATE / /

Check-in

Today's body feels

ENERGETIC
STRONG
ACHY
CAPABLE
TIRED
SLOW

Today's dominant vibe

CALM
OPTIMISTIC
OKAY
SAD
NERVOUS
SATISFIED
ANGRY
YEAH-NAH

Today's stress signals

Breathing

SLOW ○ ○ ○ FAST

Mind

CALM ○ ○ ○ RACING

Concentration

FOCUSED ○ ○ ○ DISTRACTED

Switching off

SIMPLE ○ ○ ○ CHALLENGING

Today's stress danger rating

COOL ← → HOT

Reflect

Stressful moment

Did I 'turn the story around'? How?

Bird's-eye view

Tools I used

- ☐ BREATHE
- ☐ LEAVE
- ☐ MOVE
- ☐ OTHER

Today, I am feeling good about ...

Pause

Did I do my gratitude notes?

◯ YES ◯ NO

Feeling before

Feeling after

Did I take a mindfulness pause?

◯ YES ◯ NO

Feeling before

Feeling after

Pausing improved my stress

FROM /10

TO /10

Connect

3 moments of connection

1.

2.

3.

Person I'm grateful for (and why)

Today's thank you moment

Word of the day

DAY M T W T F S S

DATE / /

Check-in

Today's body feels

- ENERGETIC
- STRONG
- ACHY
- CAPABLE
- TIRED
- SLOW

Today's dominant vibe

- CALM
- OPTIMISTIC
- OKAY
- SAD
- NERVOUS
- SATISFIED
- ANGRY
- YEAH-NAH

Today's stress signals

Breathing

SLOW ○ ○ ○ FAST

Mind

CALM ○ ○ ○ RACING

Concentration

FOCUSED ○ ○ ○ DISTRACTED

Switching off

SIMPLE ○ ○ ○ CHALLENGING

Today's stress danger rating

COOL ← → HOT

Reflect

Stressful moment

Did I 'turn the story around'? How?

Bird's-eye view

Tools I used

- ☐ BREATHE
- ☐ LEAVE
- ☐ MOVE
- ☐ OTHER

Today, I am feeling good about ...

Pause

Did I do my gratitude notes?

◯ YES ◯ NO

Feeling before

Feeling after

Did I take a mindfulness pause?

◯ YES ◯ NO

Feeling before

Feeling after

Pausing improved my stress

FROM /10

TO /10

Connect

3 moments of connection

1.

2.

3.

Person I'm grateful for (and why)

Today's thank you moment

Word of the day

DAY M T W T F S S

DATE / /

Check-in

Today's body feels

- ENERGETIC
- STRONG
- ACHY
- CAPABLE
- TIRED
- SLOW
-

Today's dominant vibe

- CALM
- OPTIMISTIC
- OKAY
- SAD
- NERVOUS
- SATISFIED
- ANGRY
- YEAH-NAH
-

Today's stress signals

Breathing

SLOW ○ ○ ○ FAST

Mind

CALM ○ ○ ○ RACING

Concentration

FOCUSED ○ ○ ○ DISTRACTED

Switching off

SIMPLE ○ ○ ○ CHALLENGING

Today's stress danger rating

COOL ← → HOT

Reflect

Stressful moment

Did I 'turn the story around'? How?

Bird's-eye view

Tools I used

- [ ] BREATHE
- [ ] LEAVE
- [ ] MOVE
- [ ] OTHER

Today, I am feeling good about ...

Pause

Did I do my gratitude notes?

◯ YES ◯ NO

Feeling before

Feeling after

Did I take a mindfulness pause?

◯ YES ◯ NO

Feeling before

Feeling after

Pausing improved my stress

FROM /10

TO /10

Connect

3 moments of connection

1.

2.

3.

Person I'm grateful for (and why)

Today's thank you moment

Word of the day

DAY M T W T F S S

DATE / /

Check-in

Today's body feels

- ENERGETIC
- STRONG
- ACHY
- CAPABLE
- TIRED
- SLOW
-

Today's dominant vibe

- CALM
- OPTIMISTIC
- OKAY
- SAD
- NERVOUS
- SATISFIED
- ANGRY
- YEAH-NAH
-

Today's stress signals

Breathing

SLOW ○ ○ ○ FAST

Mind

CALM ○ ○ ○ RACING

Concentration

FOCUSED ○ ○ ○ DISTRACTED

Switching off

SIMPLE ○ ○ ○ CHALLENGING

Today's stress danger rating

COOL ← → HOT

Reflect

Stressful moment

Did I 'turn the story around'? How?

Bird's-eye view

Tools I used

- [ ] BREATHE
- [ ] LEAVE
- [ ] MOVE
- [ ] OTHER

Today, I am feeling good about ...

Pause

Did I do my gratitude notes?

YES NO

Feeling before

Feeling after

Did I take a mindfulness pause?

YES NO

Feeling before

Feeling after

Pausing improved my stress

FROM /10 TO /10

Connect

3 moments of connection

1.

2.

3.

Person I'm grateful for (and why)

Today's thank you moment

Word of the day

DAY M T W T F S S

DATE / /

Check-in

Today's body feels

- ENERGETIC
- STRONG
- ACHY
- CAPABLE
- TIRED
- SLOW

Today's dominant vibe

- CALM
- OPTIMISTIC
- OKAY
- SAD
- NERVOUS
- SATISFIED
- ANGRY
- YEAH-NAH

Today's stress signals

Breathing

SLOW ○ ○ ○ FAST

Mind

CALM ○ ○ ○ RACING

Concentration

FOCUSED ○ ○ ○ DISTRACTED

Switching off

SIMPLE ○ ○ ○ CHALLENGING

Today's stress danger rating

COOL ← → HOT

Reflect

Stressful moment

Did I 'turn the story around'? How?

Bird's-eye view

Tools I used

- ☐ BREATHE
- ☐ LEAVE
- ☐ MOVE
- ☐ OTHER

Today, I am feeling good about ...

Pause

Did I do my gratitude notes?

◯ YES ◯ NO

Feeling before

Feeling after

Did I take a mindfulness pause?

◯ YES ◯ NO

Feeling before

Feeling after

Pausing improved my stress

FROM /10 TO /10

Connect

3 moments of connection

1.

2.

3.

Person I'm grateful for (and why)

Today's thank you moment

Reflection

Thinking about your daily check-in with your body, did you notice any patterns emerging in how you felt?

Reflect on how this journalling process may have helped you manage stress. Do you feel less anxious? Do you have more tools to manage stress?

Go back through the connection section of your journal. Use the space below to write down all the people you felt grateful for over the 90 days. (Feels good, hey?)

Reflect on the process of writing your gratitude notes. Do you think it helped interrupt your need to check your socials? Will you continue with this practise or choose another for the same purpose?

Notes

Notes

Notes

‘What you’re supposed to do when you don’t like a thing is change it. If you can’t change it, change the way you think about it.’

MAYA ANGELOU